HOW TO BE A MAN

Scenes from a Protracted Boyhood

ALSO BY THOMAS BELLER

The Sleep-Over Artist

Seduction Theory

Before and After:
Stories from New York
(editor)

HOW TO BE A ★ MAN

Scenes from a Protracted Boyhood

THOMAS BELLER

W. W. NORTON & COMPANY

NEW YORK LONDON

Some of the essays in this book have previously appeared, usually in a different form, in the following publications: "Manhattan Ate My Car" in *Slate*, "The Costume Party" in *Vogue*, "Mother Goes to Hollywood" in *The New Yorker*, "Chemistry Set" in *Cabinet*, "The Drummer" in *The New Yorker*, "The Birthday Suit" in the *New York Times Magazine*, "Portrait of the Bagel as a Young Man" in *Personals* and the *Anchor Essay Annual, 1999*, "The Problem with T-shirts" in *The New Yorker*, "A Biker in the City" in *The New Yorker*, "Turtles in New York" in the *New York Press*, "The Breakup" in *Elle*, "The Tryout" in the *New York Times* Sunday Sports section, "Addicted to Love" in *Elle*, "The Last Days of Shakespeare & Company" in the *New York Observer*, "Strip Club" in *Men's Health*, "A Car Is Not a Castle" in *Best Life*, "Scenes from a Playground," "A Bike Messenger in the City," and "The Floating Armoire" in the *New York Times* City section, and "Walking the Dog" in the *Southwest Review*.

For information about permission to reproduce selections from this book, write to Permissions, W. W. Norton & Company, Inc., 500 Fifth Avenue, New York, NY 10110

Manufacturing by The Haddon Craftsmen, Inc.
Book design by Lovedog Studio
Production manager: Anna Oler

Library of Congress Cataloging-in-Publication Data

Beller, Thomas.
How to be a man : scenes from a protracted boyhood / Thomas Beller.—1st ed.
      p.   cm.
ISBN 0-393-32683-7 (pbk.)
1. Beller, Thomas. 2. Beller, Thomas—Childhood and youth. 3. Authors, American—20th century—Biography. I. Title.
PS3552.E3364Z466 2005
813'.54—dc22
                                    2005015095

W. W. Norton & Company, Inc.
500 Fifth Avenue, New York, N.Y. 10110
www.wwnorton.com

W. W. Norton & Company Ltd.
Castle House, 75/76 Wells Street, London W1T 3QT

1 2 3 4 5 6 7 8 9 0

TO THE LATE

WRITER AND PROFESSOR JEROME BADANES

RISK-TAKER, ADVENTURER OF LITERATURE,

THE SOUL,

AND THE CITY,

WHO MADE THE WORD

"COFFEE"

SEEM LIKE A EUPHEMISM FOR ALL THAT WAS CIVILIZED AND GOOD

AND UNDER WHOSE TUTELAGE AND WITH WHOSE

FRIENDSHIP THE FIRST PENNY-DROP MOMENT OF WRITERLY AMBITION

AND EXCITEMENT WAS EXPERIENCED BY THIS WRITER,

MY ADMIRATION AND GRATITUDE FOR

THE CONTINUED SUSTENANCE OF MEMORY,

THIS BOOK

IS DEDICATED.

"And what about all the good I have in my heart — doesn't it mean anything? Is it simply a joke? A false hope that makes a man feel the illusion of his worth? And so he goes on with his struggles. But this good is no phoney."

—SAUL BELLOW

CONTENTS

★

MANHATTAN

ATE

MY CAR

★

35 years old

A LITTLE WHILE AGO I WENT TO GET MY CAR AND found that it was not where I had left it. The car is, or was, a huge, mint-green 1977 Thunderbird; almost half of the car's considerable length was taken up by the hood, which gave it the vague air of a yacht. People often responded to it with almost visceral expressions of pleasure, such as the old man who ambled up to it at a gas station and said, "Now, that's some material! That's a car! You could build three cars these days with the material on that car!"

He said all this not so much to me as to the car itself, as though the sight of it had immediately brought him back to his former 1977 self, with whom he was now striking up a conversation.

The car's condition was, from my point of view, perfect, which is to say it was perfectly poised somewhere between being a rusted-out piece of junk and one of those mint-condition vintage numbers that, I'm sure, look great cruising their native suburban roads, but always seem decadent and a bit silly on the streets of Manhattan. The car's early life had been spent in Los Angeles, and the paint job was seriously sun-faded, giving it a slightly stoned, acid-washed appearance, and creating a shade of green that was, to put it charitably, unique. Its great advantage was that it was a car I could feel very proud of, but at the same time it was simply not a car that anyone would bother to steal. Or so I had thought.

I had left it on a dusty and out-of-the-way stretch of road across from the UPS depot near the Hudson River, where alternate-side-of-the-street parking regulations do not apply. Now it was gone, but the car's absence, while at the same time making its absence all the more glaring. A pedestrian happened to be walking down the street, and I could barely resist turning to him and saying, "Excuse me, but did you see a giant green car rolling down the street?" or something like that. I stared at the spot where I had parked the car a week or so earlier. It was now occupied by another car. I looked away. I looked back. It was still not there. I was on my bike—yes, I biked to my car, such is car ownership in no-garaged Manhattan—and eventually, though my mind could not fully grasp this new absence, I realized I couldn't keep standing there. I went home.

My girlfriend, with whom I was to be taking a weekend trip, was napping. This was a great relief. I wanted some private time to deal with this unexpected turn of events. I made various phone calls to various city agencies in the hopes that it had been towed. It had not.

Then I biked back to the spot where I had last seen my car. How irrational we are in the face of bad news! The car was not there. I had elaborate weekend plans, was meant to be picking some other people up, and so I got on the cell phone and began working on contingency schemes, which resulted in my getting a friend's car, which was located in a nearby garage. It was an Audi. Actually, it was a deceased friend's Audi. The last time I had been in it he had been driving. We had been on the way to his wedding.

I got the Audi, I drove here, I drove there, we went to the country, and the whole time, as I readjusted my posture to the Audi's bucket seat (as opposed to the living room couch provided by the Thunderbird) and got the feel of the car, I vacillated between feeling grief-stricken at the loss of my car and feeling really grief-stricken at the far larger loss of my friend whose car I was now driving. Then I chastised myself for grieving about the car at all. What do you call it when your car is stolen? A bummer?

I didn't call it anything. I got back to New York at the end of the weekend, returned the Audi, biked past the spot where I had last seen my car (still not there), and proceeded to do absolutely nothing about it. What I specifically didn't do was call the police. I told a few people who had driven in the car about it, and felt consoled by their genuine dismay that it was gone. But the days turned to weeks and still I didn't call the police. I should say here a little about the car's background in my life. I had purchased it two years earlier. It was, more or less, my first car. The purpose of getting it was to take a massive cross-country driving trip. The logic of buying a 1977 Thunderbird for a massive cross-country driving trip is, obviously, questionable, as it's not exactly an economy car in terms of mileage and, furthermore, anything that old is prone to break down, but I bought the thing in the spirit of extravagance and illogic, on a lark, for fun and adventure, and as there was nothing particularly prudent or wise or rational in my decision to buy a car—one certainly doesn't need one in Manhattan—I merrily abandoned those principles when choosing which car to buy.

The car proceeded, within days of my setting off on the trip, to break down (in the middle of the night, in the middle of nowhere) and required massive engine work that in one stroke doubled the $1,000 price tag I had paid. After that it raced through eight thousand miles of American landscape in stellar form, including scaling the Rockies and an absurdly steep mountain road in Glacier National Park, though for the entire trip I was in a state of paranoia, desperately listening for that death rattle that would signify another breakdown.

At the end of this trip I became an urban car owner and commenced the bizarre Manhattan rituals of alternate-side-of-the-street parking, which so exhausted me after a while that I garaged the thing out of town for half a year and went back to having a rational urban existence of bicycles, taxis, and subways. Then, in rapid succession, I finished a novel, I brought the Thunderbird back into action, I had a triple play of bad news, I spent a month in the country walking around frozen lakes in a state of convalescent zombiedom, and then I was in New York, it was the new year (the New Millennium!), and the city was blanketed with snow.

Unusual weather often fades quickly from memory, but I

will always remember the weather of January 2000. Snow was piled in drifts along the streets, sanitation trucks were outfitted with plows and groaned up and down the avenues, alternate-side-of-the-street parking was suspended, and I had an incredible time with the Thunderbird. I parked it anywhere and everywhere. I ferried people around from here to there; it moved with majestic confidence across the snowy roads. It was never a car one wanted to rush around in—quite the opposite, its feel was always languorous and yachtlike—but now, in the snow, its ease and girth took on new dimensions. As long as I was in that car, I was safe in my own head. Outside it was a different matter.

That January 2000 I was possessed with an incredible sense of anger and prerogative. I can't explain how it worked, really, except to say it was a kind of adrenaline response to grief. There was a lot of drinking and smoking. I felt like all bets were off. The stock market was so far up it was like it was stoned. The century was supposed to end with a computer-related collapse, but that didn't happen. I had finished a book with no idea what to do next. And in the preceding month or so I had lost three people close to me, one of whom—the one who meant the most—had once turned to me and blurted out, "I have a thing about threes!"

Each left in his or her own way—there was a breakup with a woman which was like the longest, slowest removal of a Band-Aid ever, each torn follicle its own little death; there was a close friend's ceremonious bonfire of his former self and his former friendships, around which he danced spastically in a feast of acrimony and sanctimony; and then there was a death—the silent, mostly accidental, infinitely ironic but beyond irony death of an even closer friend. The night he died he had called me, inviting me to a rock and roll show, but I was busy. What I ended up being busy with was pushing the stalled car out of traffic on Sixth Avenue.

Into this emotionally whited-out void of January came all that snow, and the days of driving everywhere all the time.

I report all this as a way of explaining the fact that weeks went by without my reporting the theft of my car to the police. The car had been the seat of my well-being. That fate had swiped it from me could only be seen as a bad sign.

FINALLY, after several weeks, I went to the Sixth Precinct on Charles Street and filled out all the forms. A somewhat harried but kind black lady took down all the information, scolded me about my delay in reporting the matter, and, when I muttered, "I can't believe anyone would want to steal that car," replied with a brassy cheer I much appreciated, "Honey, if it has wheels on it, it's more than what they had."

And there should have ended the saga of my Thunderbird. The lady at the Sixth Precinct told me that an "alert" would be "put out" on my car. I imagined the alert extended into the distant future, a kind of radio signal extending parallel to many other signals that were doomed never to find the thing to which they had been alerted.

I got around town on my bike, which was my normal mode of transport, and waxed philosophical about the whole episode. I tried to feel that the car's disappearance was really a liberation; the world didn't need another car, New York least of all. It was a possession. You could replace a possession. There were other things you could not replace.

Then late one night, having biked across the Brooklyn Bridge and wound my way arbitrarily through the twisted streets of downtown Manhattan, I saw, out of the corner of my eye, a familiar-looking shape far down a dark street. The shape was a fender that had briefly caught the light. I slowed the bike and thought, No! Do not become one of those people who go down every darkened street searching for the thing they have lost. Get on with it!

I let the bike roll on but then circled back around. I was obviously destined to be one of those people who go down every darkened street searching for the thing they have lost. I approached the familiar-looking object and, to my surprise and even consternation, it only became more familiar-looking.

There sat my car. A month had gone by since I'd last seen it. It was a bit dusty but otherwise unharmed. There were no parking tickets on it, but there was a weathered piece of paper stuck under the windshield wiper. It was a note on New York Police Department stationery explaining that the car had been relocated to make way for a parade. I looked up and realized I was on the other side of the massive UPS building. I stood there for a while, touching the hood of the car, running my hands over its dusty contours, in a state of disbelief. I was so happy, but I was annoyed, too. This was not supposed to happen. When something is lost, it does not pop up again. I think on some deeper level I was thinking: Of all the things that have gone away, if I could have just one of them back, this would not be it!

★

★ ★

THERE was one more episode with the police, in which I had to go report the car unstolen. The procedure for this is that you must show up with the title, identification, and the car, and a police officer has to examine you and the car and the paperwork all at once; there was the inevitable foul-up with the paperwork, and so I found myself standing in the drizzling rain while the officer stared at the car and at the paperwork in his hand and eventually declared, "This isn't your car. Your car is a Honda," at which point I was led back into the station house and made to sit next to a man handcuffed to a bench. I was briefly a suspect in the theft of my own car.

And now I am again the owner of a 1977 Thunderbird. But though I'm happy to have it, I can't help but think of the period of its absence as the break in a fever of some kind, and its return as an allegory for something. Perhaps it's just an allegory for why one ought not to have a car in Manhattan.

The Thunderbird does have its pleasures, though. Just today I drove out to Newark airport and picked up my girlfriend, and we rumbled back into the city with a tremendous sunset at our backs. She slid over on the front seat and pressed against me. Back in Manhattan, I parked down by Center Street, in the shadow of the courthouse, with its many steps, and we walked past the jail and the bail bondsman and the shuttered shops of Sunday night Baxter Street and had a great Vietnamese dinner on Mulberry Street. Then I drove her home, dropped her off with the bags, and went in search of a parking place. I headed straight for that bereft and dusty stretch of road across from the UPS depot where alternate-side-of-the-street parking regulations do not apply. Happily, I found a spot.

THE
COSTUME
PARTY

★

13 years old

IF YOU GROW UP IN AN APARTMENT BUILDING IN New York, the building itself becomes a kind of ship, labyrinthine and ripe for exploration, and all your friends' apartments are like cabins you navigate, while the vicissitudes of the world remain outside. My best friend in the building, when I was thirteen, was a boy named Rick. The two of us formed a gang of sorts, and for years I treated his parents' apartment as an extension of my own.

My household was quiet and compact, consisting of myself, my mother, a lot of antiques, and the strange heavy/lightness of a household made both roomier and closer by the death, at the end of my ninth year, of my father. Rick's place, in contrast, buzzed with the pulse of the new: push-button phones, IBM Selectric typewriters, aerodynamic furniture, Betamax video players. There were always new people, too, his father's assistants, friends, gurus. When we were younger, a whole room had been devoted to a jungle gym for him and his sister. It was equipped with a stereo that had a big box of colored lights that throbbed in time to the music. It was a psychedelic disco for the building's kiddie generation, and I remember being ushered into this room at the age of six or so and meeting in one fell swoop all the people who would over the years be my gang in the building.

Rick's place was on the same floor as my own, and so, from proximity and affinity, we became inseparable. On weekends I often slept over, and on Sunday mornings would join the family in their orange Volkswagen for expeditions to Chinatown.

The man behind all this magic was Rick's father, Mr. Lehman, a handsome, charismatic figure whose smile and style were larger than life. He was always optimistic, always in a good mood. So I was taken by surprise when I came over one day to discover him and Rick's mother having a fight. Mr. Lehman had long black hair and a beard back then, and almost always wore all white. His mother was blond, her hair parted in the center. She often wore scarves around her neck. I thought of them as a dream of ease and pleasure, but that day they screamed at each other. I had never seen grown-ups yell like that. Their teeth flashed, a new kind of white. Rick's mom was beautiful and kind, a beauty queen from North Carolina whose lightness seemed a perfect complement for the darker intensity of her husband.

At the time, I forgot about their fight as soon as I got to

Rick's room. And so I was shocked when, some time after that, Rick's parents split up.

The kids were split up, by choice: Rick's sister went to live with her mother a few blocks away, and Rick stayed with his father. I felt bad for Rick and his younger sister, and privately mourned his beautiful mother's departure from the building. Rick's apartment now turned into a kind of two-man, multi-generational bachelor pad.

About a year or so after the divorce, a young woman started showing up with increasing regularity at Rick's apartment. She was southern, very tall and slim, with a caressing, flirtatious voice. I was thirteen. She was not a peer of mine. But she didn't exactly belong to the realm of parents, either. I found out her name was Rosie, and that she was a model, which I imagined meant she stood very still in crowded rooms where people came up and ogled her as though they were visiting a museum. She had a lot of curly blond hair. It was layered, wild, and a bit out of control, which was how I thought of her. Even when she opened the front door and found me standing there in socks, she treated me like the first guest to arrive at a party.

Rick's response to the new addition to the house was to have a lock installed on the door to his room.

OUT of fealty to Rick, I tried to maintain a certain coolness toward Rosie, and to the idea of his father and Rosie as a couple (even though they were by now living together), but despite my best efforts to resist, she won me over. By sheer virtue of proximity, she became part of my life. When Rick's dad took me along on a family vacation in the Caribbean, I walked in on her naked while she was putting her hair up in a bun. The sliding door was open, just a thick curtain hanging down, and I burst through it with a question about something. I got about three words of the question out and then stopped dead in my tracks.

"*Thomas*," she said in that southern lilt, a little scolding, and kept fiddling with her hair, unperturbed, while I stood frozen, taking in my first naked woman, before turning on my heels.

That was the trip's most sensational moment. The trip's most emotional moment, however, came late one night when Mr. Lehman came downstairs and found me rummaging in the kitchen cabinets for a midnight snack. I still remember the sight of his bare feet coming down the open staircase. There was so much of the force of his personality in his feet, and they were coming for me. I froze like a sleepwalker who has woken up to find himself somewhere he had no intention of being, in this case on a midnight raid of the kitchen. I was a fat kid, you see, and at the start of the trip Mr. Lehman, a health food nut, had given me a pep talk about how I was going to eat healthy things and swim in the ocean, and how much better I would feel. When he came padding downstairs in bare feet and caught me red-handed with all the cabinets open, I felt I had let him down. He wasn't mad, though. We had a nice talk. He assured me I didn't need to eat at this hour, and everything would be fine if I just went back to bed, which I did.

I THOUGHT Rosie was nice, but Rick remained unconvinced, so I tried to pretend otherwise. His father now had two opposing camps in his home, his girlfriend and his son, and he did his best to accommodate both. To the eclectic chaos of the apartment was added a piano room where Rosie could practice her music. Rick changed the lock on his door to something more elaborate, requiring a key on both the inside and outside. Shortly after this new lock was installed, we found ourselves madly jiggling a key to the door that would not turn. No one else was in his house. We were inside his room. Rick had left the key to the inside of the room outside, and only had the key to the outside of the room, which did not work on the inside. We had put ourselves under house arrest.

The solution was to call our dear friend Pedro, the doorman. We dropped the outside key down in a towel. There was Pedro, sprinting down Riverside Drive in the dark. His round body moved with uncharacteristic haste. He seemed oddly two-dimensional, seen from fourteen floors above. The flat surface of his doorman hat obscured his face and most of his body. He picked up the wrapped towel like it was a fumbled football and raced back up the street to his post. He locked the front door of the building, got into the apartment, and freed us. We were delighted.

None of this—the lock, the key—seemed strange to me, for some reason. It was just one of the many Byzantine necessities required to deal with the world. We spent a lot of time in Rick's room, doing nothing that required a locked door, and staging guerrilla raids on the fridge, which was always well stocked, though mostly with health food.

★ ★

★

ONE night found me dressed up for Halloween and hanging out in the lobby talking with Pedro. Rick wasn't around, having gone to stay with his mother. I was thirteen and thought of myself as worldly, but I hadn't been able to resist going trick-or-treating one last time. Part of it was the lure of the candy. And part of it was my costume, which I liked. A few years earlier, while exploring the seemingly inexhaustible closet where my mother stored things, I had found a black top hat. It was an antique, impressively sinister in shape. Its black felt surface was smooth to the touch. The closet also miraculously provided a tuxedo, from a dance performance my mother had once been a part of. In subsequent years my Halloween costume consisted of painting my face in whiteface and wearing this outfit, which made me look like a cross between an undertaker and the guy who ran the circus.

That night's takings had been meager. I was a tall kid, which meant that whenever I yelled, "Trick or treat!" I was at eye level with the grown-ups standing in the door. For the first time, I had detected alarm, or at least distaste, flash across their faces at the sight of me. As I chatted with Pedro, trying to lift my bad mood by eating a steady supply of Candy Corn and Milk Duds, the elevator door opened and out stepped Rick's dad in a blue velvet blazer, with a white silk scarf draped around his neck. He was with Rosie, whose blond hair unfurled in chaotic waves around her shoulders, enormous and weightless. Clearly they were heading for a night on the town.

"Oh, man, you look *great!*" said Rick's father, always the enthusiast.

"You look so handsome! All dressed up!" said Rosie, her Texas twang filling the marble lobby. "Look at that fantastic *hat!*"

"It's my Halloween costume," I explained, as though this needed explaining.

They said they were going to a party and invited me to come along. They said it so naturally it was as though the party in question were going to be filled with tall kids in whiteface wearing top hats. Despite feeling a pang about Rick, there was no point resisting the warmth of their praise, the excitement of their invitation.

The party was on the East Side, at the home of Eileen Ford. It was not a costume party, though everyone was dressed up. There were a few men around, in suits or turtleneck sweaters, but women dominated the room. They all seemed to be wearing creased slacks and shirts in rust, silver, and beige that had a metallic shimmer. There was a sleekness to their hair, a buffed smoothness to their skin, an unhurried languor to their movements that was different from the world of harried grown-ups I had known so far. I particularly recall their shirts—many of them had a satiny sheen, and most were unbuttoned at the top few buttons. But there was no cleavage. They were all tall, rail-thin, beautiful, cigarettes smoldering between poised, manicured fingers. They were models, but I didn't know that at the time. I only knew I had discovered a city full of adults whose identity revolved around something other than being a parent. The whole thing seemed like a perfectly natural extension of Halloween.

I got separated from Rick's father and Rosie, and found myself wandering around and talking to people. They greeted me warmly, as though I were the entertainment. "Hello!" I said to one group after another, and they all seemed glad to see me. There was a minute or two of small talk ("That's such a fantastic hat!" "Thank you. I got it from my mother's closet. She once used it in a dance performance. She's a modern dancer") and then I drifted off to another group. I felt the quiet confidence of someone doing a good job. It was like trick-or-treating, except instead of candy, I got compliments.

I was having a great time until an older woman appeared before me, stern-faced, wearing a floral print dress that was the most conservative thing in the room. She jerked her thumb toward the door. "You," she said. "Out?"

This was Eileen Ford, my host. We shook hands somewhat awkwardly, given that I was wearing a lot of whiteface makeup, a top hat and had just been asked to leave. I explained how I got to the party, but the logic of it didn't seem to impress her. Then a man appeared by her side and introduced himself as her husband. He seemed to take a kindlier view of my presence. Eventually she wandered off and Gerry Ford and I had a nice chat. I don't remember how I got home.

Not long after that party, I was roaming the eclectic bounty of Rick's house when a copy of *Vogue* caught my eye. I paused over it, and after a moment I realized with a shock that it was Rosie herself looking out at me, her green-blue eyes peering mischievously from under the brim of a straw hat. Her long index finger was suggestively poised on her lower lip, like she'd been caught stealing. It was a face I knew well, and also one unfamiliar to me. It belonged to the world I had glimpsed at that party, a world of beautiful men and women in shiny shirts, cradling cigarettes in elegant fingers.

Childhood occurs in rooms—your own, your parents', your friends'. For a while these rooms are the world, and everything outside them is scenery. But then the balance shifts and you understand the finiteness of your childhood arrangements, and that your life will take place elsewhere. My friendship with Rick was rooted in the world of our apartments, and when our lives moved outside of our homes, the friendship didn't move with it.

Quite a few years later I bumped into Rosie in the street. By then I had drifted away from Rick, and though I didn't know the exact date or circumstances of her departure, I knew she had moved out. We exchanged warm hellos, and she remarked on how much I had changed and I remarked on how little she had, at least in appearance. It was such an innocent, pleasant encounter it was hard to remember it had been her picture that I had stared at that day with such fascination, as though it were forbidden fruit, before hurrying back to Rick and the safety of his room, feeling like I had somehow betrayed him.

MOTHER
GOES TO
HOLLYWOOD

★

26 years old

IN APRIL 1992, I WAS IN LOS ANGELES PREPARING to go to the Academy Awards as the date of someone who had been nominated for an Oscar—my mother. The Oscars are about Hollywood, about bright, ephemeral glamour, about surfaces that reflect. My mother is not about these things. Yet there we were, an unlikely pair, preparing for our big night.

My mother had spent the previous ten years working on a documentary film entitled *The Restless Conscience*, which examined the resistance to Hitler inside of Germany. Most of those years were solitary, with little in the way of financial or moral support from the world at large, and for a time my mother's commitment to the movie had overtones of Don Quixote. Suddenly we were on a plane to Los Angeles, perusing the Coca-Cola Academy Award insert in *People* magazine, which dutifully listed in the Best Documentary Feature category *The Restless Conscience*. To recall the tone of the previous ten years, and to contemplate the substance of the movie itself, which was not about surfaces that reflect, and to contrast that to this glossy advertisement in *People* and all that lay before us just then—all this had the effect of broadening one's sense of what is possible in the world.

We arrived several days in advance and my mother set herself up in the Beverly Hilcrest Hotel while I went off to stay with a friend. The Beverly Hilcrest Hotel was almost certainly a glamorous hotel at one time, but that time had passed. My mother's room was enormous, with a great view, and yet it had a vaguely decayed quality. The color scheme was what could best be described as "mustard." There were floor-to-ceiling drapes, slightly frayed, and I found them heartbreaking for some reason. Whenever I visited her in that hotel room she seemed small.

The big day arrived at last and I went to pick up my mother, wearing a new tuxedo I had purchased for the occasion. It itched. Having briefly considered hiring a limousine, we prudently decided on a taxi instead. Our taxi pulled up to the hotel curb with a wheeze. It was not luxurious. We got in and then we remembered to give the driver the piece of paper with said, "Academy Awards, please." There was a long pause, and the address on it.

As we approached the venue, I noticed that the population of limousines on the street was increasing. Eventually there was nothing but limousines, all extra long and of various shades of gray, blue, black, and white, and they were all stuck in traffic. It was like the display floor of an enormous car dealership specializing in stretch limousines. In the midst of the limousines was our taxi, which was blue, except for the hood, which was orange, and which seemed to have been built in a different era than the rest of the car.

My mother and I had heard that it was customary for people to circle the venue in their limousines, waiting until just the right moment to arrive. But no one was circling now. No one was moving, in fact. It was three in the afternoon, and the starting time was a half hour away. After a little while a few people began to get out of their limousines and walk. Gradually more and more people started walking. It was like one of those old movies where there is a panic about an impending nuclear war or the arrival of Godzilla, and everyone takes to the highway, and when that gets jammed, they start to flee on foot. In this instance people were fairly calm and matter-of-fact about it. No one was going to let this traffic jam ruin their day. The doors to all the limousines opened up and out came calm, well-dressed men and women wearing fabulous shoes that weren't made for walking. My mother and I got out as well.

Eventually we got to a point where there was a density of police. I went up to one of them and asked directions.

"Could you tell me where the entrance to the Academy Awards is?" I said.

The policeman was wearing mirrored sunglasses. Several seconds went by. It is hard to convey skepticism while wearing mirrored sunglasses, but the policeman managed to do it.

"My mother is nominated for an award," I said. I gestured to my mother, as if her presence were some kind of proof.

Another moment went by. Then, as if we had passed some test, he pointed up a hill. There was a mob of people there, and a fire truck.

"Of course," I said. "Thank you."

The entrance to the Academy Awards was a bit daunting. A red carpet cut through a canyon of bleachers crammed with people, all of whom seemed to have cameras. We showed our tickets and stepped forward, and all at once the cameras started to whiz and chirp. It was like listening to locusts devour a forest. My mother held my arm, and we marched solemnly down the red-carpeted aisle as though I were giving her away at a wedding. I wondered if people were taking our picture, and then I realized that the man a few feet in front of us was Kevin Costner. I held up a moment to let him get farther ahead, and then we went on, down through the valley of the locusts.

My mother and I entered the sight lines and consciousness of hundreds of people, all of whom had cameras pressed to their faces. I could feel their viewfinders bearing down on us. Memories were scanned and calculations made. A second went by, maybe less, and then all those hundreds dropped their cameras to their chests simultaneously, a chorus line of disappointed fans and paparazzi.

My mother and I continued down the red carpet, looking at the palm trees that had been brought in for atmosphere, at the disappointed paparazzi, and at each other. My tuxedo itched mercilessly. The palm trees, I decided, were fake. My mother was wearing quite a bit of makeup, which was unusual for her, and I found this unnerving. She had gone to a special place to have her face made up, appropriate for the occasion, I thought, except now her expression was slightly distorted. A wave of sadness came over me. I felt as though we had become unmoored from ourselves. We smiled at each other and she squeezed my arm and I recognized her again.

Then something revived the paparazzi's interest, and the locusts began their frenzy again. My mother and I stopped for a moment, stunned, I think, and we turned around to see Daryl Hannah taking what appeared to be bows in the manner of royalty when they are in the presence of their subjects. She looked regal, wearing a golden dress, and with lots of blond hair done up like Marilyn Monroe. The sun was setting, and it was very pretty.

The awards themselves were like a game show with very attractive contestants. I thought about the people in my mother's movie—their concern for ethics, their sense that actions have consequences—and how odd it was that they should in some way be here, in a place filled with tuxedos and chiffon dresses.

The presenters for the Best Documentary category were Spike Lee and John Singleton. They took turns reading off the names of the nominees, and as each name was mentioned a brief clip of the film was shown, selected by the Academy, not the directors of the movies. My mother and I had spent a fair amount of time speculating which five seconds, out of two hours, they might choose to run. As it happened they ran a shot of Hitler and then a quick shot of a Nazi flag. My mother had gone to great lengths to keep Hitler offstage in the movie; he was a supporting character, not the main event, but there he was anyway, our little contribution to however many million people were watching: another shot of that bad guy.

But there was no time to worry about this because the

announcement was at hand, and besides, in reciting the nominees John Singleton had just mispronounced our last name. It's "Beller," and he said it "Belyer." No big deal, I thought—the guy is under a lot of pressure, he's reading from a teleprompter, it's his first time on the Oscars, there are bigger things to worry about in the world. And yet several hundred million people had just fleetingly apprehended our last name incorrectly.

Then came the envelope. When we arrived my mother had been disturbed by the fact that we were not on the aisle, where she thought the winners would be seated. I assured her that this wasn't the case, that only two very secretive accountants knew who had won, and that they would never do something so obvious as seat the winners where they could most conveniently get to the stage.

Now Spike fumbled with the envelope, and my mother clutched a carefully folded piece of paper—an acceptance speech that she had spent the last several days working on. She had been told that all acceptance speeches had to be under forty-five seconds, or else, and so she had devoted a great deal of time in her huge mustard-colored hotel room creating a text that was filled with gratitude and emotion, conveyed a message, included thanks to about twenty people, and could be delivered without any haste in less than forty-five seconds. Spike finally had the piece of paper out of the envelope and a great hush came over the hall.

Even the most ardent Oscar enthusiasts probably don't care much about the Best Documentary Feature category; it may be the category with the lowest celebrity quotient. But I sensed a reverential silence as Spike and John Singleton prepared to utter the winner. This silence is a moment of truth that everyone recognizes; it is, I think, like a window through which you can climb for just a moment, into a place where you can pretend to be the one on the edge of his seat. In this case, pretending wasn't necessary.

"And the Oscar goes to . . ." Spike said. I glanced sidewise at my mother, whose hands were clasped over her speech. Her face was stern, almost grim. For ten years everything that happened to this movie happened because she willed it to, yet now, of course, we had no say in the matter. The dice were in midair. Singleton read the name of the winners, and whoops and cries of joy erupted from the aisle seats at the end of our row.

The winners made their speech, and then it was time for the next category. It all seemed so odd—the importance of the event wildly magnified and simultaneously diminished by that game show atmosphere, the big monitors, the surreal dresses. I sneaked a peek at my mother. She sat there completely still, her face impassive and without expression, or so it would have seemed to someone else. To me, there was a lot going on in that face. Her hands still clutched the speech. She was clutching it so hard the piece of paper trembled a little. I didn't know quite what to do, and it was then that the man sitting on the other side of her, a documentary filmmaker named Vince DiPersio, who had been nominated for two Oscars now and had been runner-up twice, turned to her quite suddenly and gave her a big kiss on the cheek. He had a beard, and I imagined the bristles of his beard touching her skin. It was as if something melted, and a more familiar expression came over her face. She turned to him and we all laughed. At that moment my mother's face *was* a surface that reflected, and the light surrounding her was wonderfully illuminating.

CHEMISTRY SET

★

10 years old

CHEMISTRY SET. WHAT A HAPPY-MAKING PAIR OF words! And within the chemistry set, test tubes filled with strange-colored powders, including a finely sifted substance that was pitch-black and that, once I removed the cork at the top, immediately got everywhere onto everything and was impossible to remove.

It's possible I'm confusing this with the finger-printing set, but I don't think so (or maybe it happened twice). Along with the chemistry set came the whole ambience of a chemist—someone wearing a white laboratory coat, who takes notes on graph paper, who peers into bubbling beakers from which little puffs of white smoke rise. The chemist is like a magician. He's a person who, using known quantities, the facts of the physical world, can create unknown quantities, new substances, or, at the very least, some kind of explosion. Or, at the very least, some memorably nasty-smelling concoction.

MY father brought me the chemistry set from someplace far away. He'd been on a trip. Back then everything that wasn't home was far away. From faraway places came gifts. At the end of an absence, a present. The gifts varied in shape and size. From Philadelphia he brought me a jigsaw puzzle. I spilled it out on the floor, and it stayed there, a reproach, a mess. I eventually put it back in the box. I never did the puzzle, but I loved getting the present, the exchange of kisses, getting all excited, his sandpaper cheek against my smooth one—he lifts me off the ground.

From where did he bring the chemistry set? I can't recall. But I loved it right away. My father was a doctor. I knew this had some tangential relationship with chemistry. Both disciplines involved men in white smocks, test tubes, experiments, charts. My father was a psychoanalyst. I didn't quite understand what this meant. I still don't, entirely. But I sensed that it was connected to chemistry in a strange, abstract way.

As excited as I was by the ambience of precision, it was only an ambience. A feeling. I had no discipline. I couldn't concentrate. I liked to throw things out of windows. I was a consumer of textures: the coarse granulated texture of Nestlé chocolate milk mix, which I fed into my mouth in heaping tablespoon portions on which I nearly choked. The fine, melting, velvety texture of powdered sugar, which I fed into my mouth in heaping tablespoon portions on which I nearly choked. The wonderfully bland superfine powder of straight flour, which I fed into my mouth in heaping tablespoon portions on which I nearly choked. I probably wasn't the ideal kid for a chemistry set. Already the tests had begun. At the age of seven I saw a neurologist. "He'll need a secretary just like me," he said, by way of explaining my handwriting, why it was bad, and I had jumped around merrily in the waiting room, made more happy by that strangely concerned look on my parents' faces. Now I'm fond of that memory because it's proof my slide began back when there were still two of them.

I THOUGHT of the neurologist's remark a few years later when seated with old Mr. Murphy, the handwriting teacher. His kind smile, hooded blue eyes, and very jowly cheeks made his face look a bit turkey-ish. The kindliness with which he received me into his office was heartbreaking, and even at eleven I wanted to say, "Don't even try to help me, it'll discourage you," when he gave me that hearty but tender hello of his.

I was by then a connoisseur of the dead silence of hallways. Behind closed doors classes took place, but for a variety of reasons I was often in the hall, waiting out the punishment, or en route to some little office. These were the days when I made the rounds of little offices at my school: the assistant principal, the school psychologist, the math tutor, the English tutor. I was a special case. I was given blocks to play with on their desks while we chatted. I was an expert at these interpretive games, but my handwriting was as legible as a Rorschach test. I needed a handwriting coach, and Mr. Murphy was that man.

They were letting him hang around after retirement to work with the special cases. His eyes, on cold wintry days, watered like crazy. If it weren't for his smile I would have thought Mr. Murphy was crying. I knew he was not because, although I disliked being with him indoors, I was always happy to see him roaming the campus on bright wintry days in his gray flannel overcoat, his hat, his black gloves, his wobbling turkey smile, and his cheeks streaming with tears. Mr. Murphy's watery eyes were a refuge amid an otherwise forbidding place. He was the only other person moving as slow as me. Indoors, he persevered with the handwriting lessons. He was equipped with plastic sheets on which each letter was stenciled out in delicate legible script, and I was to follow the stencil with my own pen. Penmanship, that was Mr. Murphy's subject. His salt-and-pepper hair was combed straight back. For some reason my memories of him are of very cold days, black leather gloves, and crying eyes. When I think back to those teachers of mine when I was eleven and twelve years old, I feel sad that I was so oblivious to their gifts of attention and hope. But grateful, too. I needed those people.

In Mr. Murphy's office the walls were lined with old photographs of the school's teaching staff assembled like a basketball team, tall guys like Mr. Murphy in the back. The earliest picture with Mr. Murphy in it was from the forties. But I'm exaggerating on Mr. Murphy's behalf; he didn't have an office, they were indulging his desire to do something, I think—we were both marginal characters at the school, that was part of our bond—and we met in a slightly musty board-room with floral couches along the walls and a long polished table in the center where the trustees occasionally met and where disciplinary committees were often held. In subsequent years, when brought before various tribunals in that same room, I would think it was lucky Mr. Murphy wasn't around to see me like this, accused of crimes against his school. Sitting beside him and his raspy breathing, I would follow the stencil and then trace it on my own on a piece of paper with the letter already written out, and finally all on my own, a barely legible scribble.

"Oh, no," he would say, "that's not quite it. Here, you want to . . ." and he would demonstrate an S, a very nice black fountain pen in his hand that, though it shook and flapped and seemed barely in his control, always settled down for his demonstration of how to write with penmanship. How the hell did I get to Mr. Murphy? Maybe I just think of him as part of that chemistry set era.

THE chemistry set was handled carefully at first. The things my father brought me were highly prized. We had secrets, he and I, secret understandings, such as when we would without warning fling a balled-up napkin at one another in the middle of dinner. I always assumed that these gifts had a place in that secret unarticulated dialogue of ours, even if I didn't know exactly what they meant. Plus, I liked presents.

But I liked getting them more than I liked having them. Along with the mad scientist vibe of the chemistry set comes another impulse, quite the opposite of the cold rationalist who observes phenomena and takes notes on them on graph paper, namely the impulse to experience. The impulse to put in your mouth. To ingest. To experience the physical world not from the distance of observer but to get right into it as a participant, to get all that stuff in those test tubes on your hands and fingers and smell it!

So you sit there before your newly opened chemistry set in your room. You have been instructed to follow the instructions. You make a brief attempt at understanding the instruction booklet. But it isn't long before you get around to the smelling, the handling, the tapping little bits out of the test tube into your palm, or perhaps into another test tube, for some random mixing of components.

And then you open the test tube called "Sulfur." And smell it. Almost all the other smells existed in the mouth, the back of the throat, or up behind the eyes. But sulfur goes straight to the gut. It stands apart. It's like that magic trick that appeared in your room at around the same time—the handkerchief that is a deep lustrous purple with a little loop in one corner, within which you could pull through a bright pink handkerchief, the whole thing turning itself inside out as it emerged from your fist. In it went as purple, out it came as pink! The smell of sulfur went all the way down to your gut, the place beneath your gut, all the way down, and then pulled you through your ass and turned you inside out, and oh, my God! Put that cork back in the test tube! Then stare with horror and wonder that something could smell so bad.

SICILY was the world's provider of sulfur until the end of the nineteenth century, when a new method allowed for the mining of deposits in Louisiana and Texas. Once, on a visit to Sicily, I found myself driving fast along the island's southern edge, the sea to my left and open fields of cut hay to my right. Somewhere behind me was the island's volcano, Etna, which I had visited that morning. It was not yet dusk, and the late afternoon sun slanted sharply across a field of hay and made it look enchanted. It glowed as though lit from below; the yellow-orange light was the color of sulfur, the color of a sunset.

On its own, sulfur is used in the vulcanization of rubber, in lime-sulfur sprays to destroy plant parasites, in the manufacture of artificial fertilizer and certain types of cements and electric insulators, in certain ointments and medicines, and in the manufacture of gunpowder and matches. (All this according to the *McGraw-Hill Concise Encyclopedia of Science and Technology*.)

There's a butterfly called the Orange Sulphur (*Corias eurytheme*). It's the color of a lemon drop. Another butterfly is called the Cloudless Sulphur (*Phoebis sennae*). It's the color of a creamsicle. Once you start fixating on a color, you remember it everywhere. It becomes a Zelig of colors. That bright brown earth that sat, a few years after the era of the chemistry set, in a lumpy pile next to my father's grave, ready to be poured in on top of the coffin, weren't there streaks of shitty light brown in it, bordering on yellow? Was that sulfur making a cameo?

Sulfur bubbles up in springs. When you wallow in a natural spring, the water nearly hot, the air cool, there is that faint rotten-egg sulfur smell. When a geyser erupts in Yellowstone National Park—Old Faithful, for example—you smell that smell. In Saratoga Springs, New York, you can fill a bottle of the rotten-egg-smelling water from a fountain in the public park and drink it. Many people do. They have a superstitious feeling that this water has magical properties that will help them create and digest, two similar activities. Perhaps it gives them that feeling of being pulled out through their own ass and turned inside out into the world as a new and different person.

THE
DRUMMER

29 years old

I ONCE PLAYED DRUMS IN A ROCK BAND NAMED Honus Wagner. We lasted for five years. Then we broke up and I had to reconcile myself to life without the drums. I could still play the drums by myself, which is a joy in much the same way shooting a basketball around by yourself is a joy, but it's not the same as playing in a real game. In order to console myself, I began searching for reasons that not being in a band might be a good thing.

Reasons not to be in a band: One is likely to acquire, as I have, a slight ringing in one's ears (especially if you're the drummer). One hears about money a lot but rarely sees any. Not being in a band would mean not waiting for that big break. You would no longer stagger offstage after the best show of your life, which you put everything into because the record company person was there, only to discover that the record company person was not there.

Not being in a band would mean not having to wait for your bandmates to show up at a rehearsal or a show. You would not have to wait while they tuned up. You would not have to wait until they tuned up again.

Then there are fans, whose demands can be a problem, or there are no fans, an even bigger problem.

Honus Wagner fell in between. We never made it out of the zone of having to call-pester-mail-beg our circle of friends and family to show up at the venues we played. If we didn't beg and plead for people to come, no one would come, or at least not enough to elevate the event beyond a kind of public rehearsal.

But we had fans. There was a group of people who liked our music and came to our shows. We had a guy who was a sort of super fan. His name was Walter. He was a burly, broad-chested figure with long black hair parted in the middle. He had grown up in East New York, Brooklyn, and then Ozone Park, Queens, out near JFK. Our bassist had been friends with Walter in high school, but his enthusiasm seemed to go beyond this connection. Walter showed up to almost all of our shows. He could single-handedly make a show seem like it had an enthusiastic audience. If we had a thousand Walters, we would have been in serious business. But there was only one Walter.

Success would, on the surface, solve a lot of the problems of being in a band, but no matter how successful you are, there are problems that have to do with time that cannot be solved. For example, my whole ambition, while playing in Honus Wagner, was to go on tour. I just wanted to bounce from one city to another, one hazy party situation to another, weightless, playing our songs and making faces while I pounded the drum set. We did manage to tour once. We drove cross-country from New York to Berkeley, California, where the guitarist's mom was willing to put us up for several weeks until we found a place in San Francisco. We did find a place, a crash pad full of crystal meth junkies who gathered around us in excitement to talk about our upcoming gig at a place called the I-Beam. The I-Beam, now defunct, was a bit of a legend, a huge place on Haight-Ashbury. We were the opening act for a band that had won a radio talent contest for local acts. The band was called Idiot's Delight. No one at the crash pad, including the guy who lived in the closet, had heard of Idiot's Delight, but they had certainly heard of the I-Beam. They were in bands, too. They were psyched. But they didn't come to the show. The problem, according to Roger, the most charismatic and tattooed figure there, was that he had a waking dream in which spiders were crawling all over him, so he couldn't leave the house.

WE played up and down the West Coast. We had all sorts of adventures in San Francisco, Seattle, and Los Angeles, but the high point of that tour took place in Minneapolis, where we played the Seventh Street Entry on the way out, and then, because it had gone so well, on the way back, too. Two nights!

As with many high points, it followed a low point, which occurred when we first arrived in a town on our way out West. We were booked to open for a band named the Magnolias, and had been given the name of their drummer, Tom Cook, a notoriously hospitable guy with a loft and spare couches. Cook was even more hospitable than advertised—he greeted us warmly and let us spend the night on his couches in spite of the fact that neither he nor anyone at the club had ever heard of us. But the promoter, after an initial cantankerous display of bluster, took pity on us and allowed us to play. The Magnolias were a power pop band fronted by a reedy-voiced maniac named Jon Freeman, whose day job was working at Kinko's and whose lyrics reflected this—certain phrases got repeated over and over. They were big in their hometown and the show was sold out. When you are in a band, the task of making it seems so monumental that every high point feels very high. This was not the only high point of Honus Wagner, but it was the first time we played in front of a crowd of complete strangers who seemed to like what we were doing. After that show I thought I could tour forever.

But it was after the last show in Minneapolis, on the way home, as I watched the lead singer of the headlining band order a brandy at the end of the night, that I perceived that situation's limitations. The house lights were up and the equipment was packed. He was older. His band had enjoyed a brief glow of fame that was now quickly fading and would shortly be extinguished, though the band's name surely lives on in the memory of anyone who ever heard it: Gay Bikers on Acid. He knocked back half a glass of brandy in a gulp and ordered another. I thought I glimpsed in his fatigue, his boredom, a thinness and depletion that touring for a long time might bring on, and I fathomed the rock star conundrum that getting what you are working toward does not make it all better. We never toured again, though, so I did not find out.

★ ★ ★

THE area I've been focusing on, in my attempt to dissuade myself from my rock and roll aspirations, is my instrument, the drums. Who in their right mind would want to be a drummer?

When you play the drums, even by yourself, you sometimes cannot believe you are the one who is making all this noise. It is, simultaneously, an incredible affirmation that you exist, and a kind of erasure—you are no longer there, you are out of your body altogether, lost inside a cloud of noise.

During shows I often had this weird moment in midsong, sweating and beating on the drums when I'd think, Holy shit, what do I do now? What if I just stopped? The mind panics but the body keeps on exerting itself, both propelling the music and being propelled by it, afloat in sonic density. Okay, there is that, but, I told myself, let's look at the downside.

Reasons not to be a drummer: Among all the instruments of pop music, a drum set is the most cumbersome to move, and also the least glamorous while in transit (as opposed to guitars). How weird it is to travel to shows with your drums, when there is always that awkward moment when they are on the sidewalk while you wait for your ride. It's about as natural as having your living room set on the sidewalk. These are precious objects!

And then it occurred to me that my drums were in fact *part* of the living room of my house for a while. My first rudimentary drum set was presented to me in the living room (a levitational moment of happiness I will never forget), and later, in retirement, one particular floor tom sat under the table in the foyer at my mother's place; it was a white cylinder with metal legs, and one's eyes quickly got used to glossing over it. It merged into the other details of my mother's life, and I wonder if she even noticed it in the decade or so that it sat there, and if she did, if she remembered back to those odd scenes when she came to see us play. The issue of parents at rock shows is not much discussed. But they are often there. And what did she see and think about all that? She responded to the unmistakable energy and evidence that her son was alive, I suppose.

Honus Wagner's lead singer and songwriter's mother, a frail, feisty, and dignified woman with a cane, faithfully came to every show. Afterward, in the sweaty chaotic relief of the first moments offstage, he would always rush off to attend to his mother. And so the audience, whomever was there, would see the guy who was just wailing away onstage, making all that noise, holding his mother's arm as she made her way, well-coifed hair, white raincoat, small steps through the murky neon interior of CBGB's or one of the other small clubs we played, out onto the street, where he got her a cab. Then he'd come back greatly relieved and want to spend the rest of the night with the bassist and me talking about the show.

MORE reasons not to be a drummer:

Up onstage, a rock band has license to behave as badly as they please—all except the drummer. He is the only one who must spend the whole time sitting down, as though in class. Whereas other musicians gain attention with interesting lyrics, catchy melodies, or, at the very least, an arresting stage presence, a drummer tends to get attention by being loud, bombastic, and generally having a fit not unlike a temper tantrum in which all the pots and pans in the kitchen are thrown on the floor. It's a medium that often tends toward the unsophisticated, the primal, the animal.

In fact, in the context of a rock band, the behavior of a drummer bears some resemblance to the behavior we expect and appreciate in dogs.

Dogs: reliable. Drummers: same. Dogs: fun and friendly, but capable of sudden and shocking acts of lewd behavior. Drummers: same. Dogs: playful and frolicsome until told to heel. Drummers: same. A dog will be scolded by his master for crapping on the new rug. A drummer will be scolded by the songwriter for continuing his raucous drum solo into the quiet part of the new song. (Whether or not a drummer will be scolded for actually crapping on the rug varies from one band to the next.) Then there is the sad and unnerving fact that drummers, like dogs, seem to be susceptible to sudden and unexpected fatalities involving cars, or poison, or both. The drummer for the band Motorhead has the right idea: His name is Phil but his nickname is "Philthy Animal."

Aside from Charley Watts, it would seem nearly impossible to play the drums in a rock band and have dignity. And so I try and take comfort in the fact that logic and good taste dictate that this sort of life is to be avoided. The next time you see a drummer live, throw the man a bone. Would that I could be the one there to catch it!

THE
BIRTHDAY
SUIT

★

34 years old

I ONCE HAD A GIRLFRIEND WHO BOUGHT ME CLOTHES. At first this made me extremely happy, but then something changed, and these gifts, which had seemed such a pure expression of love, began to seem like little apologies.

The first thing C gave me was a blue T-shirt that she had embroidered, while on jury duty, with a little flower—a green twisty stem topped with pink petals. "It's a sweet pea," she told me as I stared at it with astonished gratitude. The idea that she had put that much effort into something for me was exhilarating. When I put it on she gave me an appraising look. "It's a little high and to the left," she said. "But it's sweet."

C's appraising looks were not to be taken lightly.

There are some people in the world who will marvel at an object for what it is—the Appreciators. Then there are others who will see in that same object all sorts of potential for what it can become—the Improvers. C fell squarely in the latter camp.

Improvers are usually visual people who care a lot about surfaces and are able, with whatever means are available to them, to create beautiful environments in which to live. The one downside to this, from the point of view of the Appreciators, is that life sometimes requires a certain amount of stillness, of *idleness*, and the Improvers are notoriously busy. C was an architect, a profession that likes people most when they are represented as tiny nonmoving miniature objects that do not sneeze or spill or move. Not that I have anything but respect for architects.

C was a very busy woman who, when she wasn't busy being busy, was busy shopping for ways to improve her home, herself, and, eventually, her boyfriend.

After that first magnificent sweet-pea T-shirt came a green windbreaker with racing stripes down the sleeves. She found it in a thrift store for twenty-five dollars. It had a peculiar sheen to it. No item of clothing I have ever owned has elicited so many favorable comments. The T-shirt and the windbreaker quickly became prized possessions. They were followed by another T-shirt, and then a button-down shirt, and then a pair of dark green cargo pants.

I was no slouch in the gift department—I got her an abundance of flowers and books, a small Indian drawing, and, with a degree of trepidation that in hindsight should have alarmed me, an old silk Japanese robe that she politely wore once. My gifts to her were private things, directed inward, for personal use. She, in turn, was remaking my very surface.

I was glad for the attention. I was impressed by her generosity. The odd thing about the new clothes was that it wasn't as though I were being turned from a slob to a fashion plate. If anything, it was the reverse. My black leather jacket was replaced by a Carhartt. Some crisp cotton shirts with stripes from Brooks Brothers now hung beside some newly arrived check shirts from J. Crew. I was being gently nudged into the realm of slightly studied scruffiness. I came to have a visceral appreciation of the fact that the first step toward being stylish is to deemphasize style, or at least the effort of moving toward it. I liked this subtle adjustment—it was like going to the style chiropractor and getting realigned—but the gifts began to take a toll. For one thing, I began to feel that as nice as the sentiment behind the gifts was, I wanted to see the sentiment expressed in ways other than the giving of these gifts.

"I'm starting to feel like there's a complaint being lodged here," I said one day, when I came home to discover another box within which was some tissue paper within which was a shirt. "Did you really despise all my old clothes?"

"Not at all," C said, a little hurt. "I just thought you'd look nice in that shirt."

"It just seems like there's a bit of a renovation taking place," I said.

"But that's the way it's *supposed* to work between men and women," she said. "A woman sees this promising clump of clay and thinks, 'I could do something with that.'"

As was so often the case with C's remarks, this comment

required some scrutiny to determine whether it was a compliment or an insult.

On the downside, I was being called a clump of clay. On the upside, I had potential. I just needed some molding, some administering to, some pruning and grooming and so forth. Even now I'm not sure whether the insult outweighs the compliment, or vice versa. We'd all like to be told we are perfect the way we are, except that we all know we are far from perfect. We long for someone to come along and slap us into shape, right the tilting ship of our existence, and set us on the right course wearing a pair of dark green cargo pants.

But clothes given in the context of romantic love are always a bit more than pure acts of generosity. They are acts of disclosure. What is being disclosed is one person's fantasy of what the other might become, what the *pair of you* might become. (Clothes given in the context of familial love are a bit different; they're like supplies for the great trek into life that the recipient, it is understood, must make on his own.) When you give your lover a gift of clothes, it's a way of saying: This is how I want to see you.

From my end of things, I was so generally impressed with how C looked and dressed that she seemed in absolutely no need of my input on the matter beyond my fairly steady (and sincere) noises of appreciation. But one of the downsides to the Appreciators is that love (the ultimate appreciation) has within it a kernel of idiocy. This idiocy can often be seen registered on the face of the lover. Noises of appreciation are the stuff of life, but they are also curiously passive; approval is a monotone. A single thorn of criticism is usually more memorable than a hundred compliments, sadly, and the dawning realization that I was on the short end of the Pygmalion stick was a very sharp thorn.

This realization occurred on C's birthday when, to go along with the presents I had bought her, she gave one to herself: a haircut. For me! She'd been joking that I needed one, and ought to get one at a different place than my usual barber, and on her birthday she took the initiative and booked me at her own salon. She paid for it. All I had to do was show up.

The salon was on Madison Avenue. The place, it was immediately evident, specialized in the thousand-dollar just-out-of-bed look. Everyone wielding scissors was a dead ringer for Rod Stewart, in the hair department. The man who cut my hair seemed to only occasionally snip at it; mostly he stared at it very intensely, occasionally giving it a contemptuous little shove this way or that, as though he were giving it a good talking-to.

When I came out onto the street it was dusk. Madison Avenue was swarming with people bundled against the cold. The sky was a cruel and magnificent blue. I let myself be swept up in the crowd, and as I moved along I realized that I was in the grip of some strange panic. Something had been taken away from me, though I couldn't understand what. I arrived at Forty-seventh Street, the diamond district, where I turned west and began walking past window after brightly lit window filled with glittering diamond rings. I had already bought C her birthday presents, but I was suddenly convinced I had to buy her one more.

It was almost six o'clock, closing time on that street, and the windows were now filled with hands removing trays of diamond rings. The fading light and the disappearing diamonds dovetailed somehow with the sense that something in me was disappearing, too. It wasn't my identity that was going away. That would be too easy a formulation. It was my *will*, the authority that goes along with knowing what you want, that quality of certainty and decisiveness and discernment that makes a man tick.

I ducked into a tiny store, eyes watering from the cold, and pointed impulsively at a bracelet of glittering pale blue stones, something out of a fairy tale.

"Topaz," said the man behind the counter with solemn gravity. "Excellent quality." I intuited that this phrase was something of a contradiction, but I didn't care. After a brief negotiation I walked out with the thing in my pocket. It was an act of love, this bracelet, but it was also an act of retaliation, somehow. We had entered a kind of competition. Unfortunately, she won. I lost. What I lost was her.

Did I lose when I didn't fire back a dress on the heels of that embroidered T-shirt? Or maybe I lost when, in addition to being dressed by her, I began dressing *for* her. You can only dress for your lover to a certain point. Beyond that it has to be for yourself.

For my birthday, a few months later, C bought me a suit from Helmut Lang. My birthday suit! C and I had been in that store before, just after we had met, when we had wandered aimlessly around Soho and we ended up drifting in and out of each other's sight in the store's cool Hitchcockian architecture. It was quite romantic. This second visit was a more businesslike affair, and I couldn't help but feel that on some perverse level she was dressing me up to go out there and meet some other woman after she was gone. When I shared this thought with her later, she laughed and admitted it was slightly true, and that she was furious with herself in some way for having gotten it for me. In some odd way all her ambivalence got channeled into buying me clothes. Such is life's algebra, that you can get an embroidered T-shirt that sends you over the moon, and a thousand-something-dollar suit from Helmut Lang that makes you melancholy. But it was very nice of her to have gotten it for me.

PORTRAIT OF THE BAGEL AS A YOUNG MAN

★

27 years old

HIS HANDS WERE LARGE. MY RÉSUMÉ LAY FLAT ON HIS desk. He had cleared a space amid the clutter, and he ran one of those big, sensitive, but also violent-looking hands over it again and again while he studied it, as though his hand were a scanner and would impart some key bit of information that reading never could. I later discovered that this was in fact what he was doing—he couldn't read very well, and seemed to place as much importance in a document's texture as in its contents.

The boss—sitting behind an impossibly cluttered desk, in an impossibly cluttered room, with the sound of the bagel factory in full swing upstairs, churning away with the noise of a ship's engine—looked down at the résumé and chewed thoughtfully on his lower lip. Then he abruptly looked up with the penetrating, profound, and fired-up expression of a prosecutor who is about to ask the question on which the whole case would turn. He said: "If someone buys three dozen bagels, and they get a free bagel for every dozen, how many would you give them?"

I thought I heard everyone else in the room collectively catch their breath. There were five of them crammed into the tiny space. They had given me a cursory once-over when I walked in, but now I could feel their eyes upon me. I had seen the ad in the *New York Times*, and it occurred to me that I was part of a long parade of applicants that had come through the office that day. I wondered whether it had been on this question that they had stumbled, one after another.

"Thirty-nine," I said.

Mr. H didn't respond. He went back to studying my résumé, chewing his lips and running that large hand over it again and again. Then he looked up at me.

"Are you Jewish?" he said.

I LIKE bagels, but I never craved them, never viewed them as something special, out of the ordinary, or exotic. They were a fact of life, personified, when I was growing up, by the local store that baked and sold them, H&H Bagels, on Eightieth Street and Broadway, which was open twenty-four hours a day, seven days a week. Besides selling bagels, the store performed a kind of community service by perfuming the air in its vicinity with the smell of baking bread, which gave the chaotic stretch of Broadway north of Seventy-ninth

Street a neighborly, friendly feel. There is something about the smell of baking bread, in its diffuse form, that civilizes people.

Once, during an autumn college break, I was walking along Broadway late at night on the way home from a party when an unexpected snow began to fall. It was exhilarating and beautiful, and I rhapsodized about the beauty of the city and of the snow, paid careful attention to the little clumping sounds of my feet on the whitening sidewalk, and scarcely noticed that I was cold.

Then, after a few blocks, I noticed. I progressed very quickly through the various stages of cold until I felt on the verge of freezing to death. I walked faster. I had no money in my pocket for a cab, just a couple of quarters, and with each block the distance home seemed to increase.

And then, amid dark and shuttered Broadway, there appeared an oasis of light and warmth—H&H Bagels.

A lone cashier stood behind her register, white paper cap atop her head.

"What's hot?" I said.

Behind the cashier was the oven, and just then one of the bakers in his white uniform slid a wooden platter into the maw of the oven and removed a squadron of steaming plain bagels, which he dumped into a wire bin. My two cold coins were enough for a hot bit of sustenance. The bagel burned my numb fingers. I walked the rest of the way home with the warm dough permeating my senses.

It was this kind of memory—vague, nostalgic, innocent—that had sprung to mind that day in early September 1992 when, amid a bleak session of scanning the *New York Times* help-wanted ads, I came across an ad placed by a bakery that identified itself as being located on the Upper West Side.

I looked up and thought, What other bakery is located on the Upper West Side? And then I ran to a fax machine with my résumé.

At that time I was a fledgling writer with a graduate degree, a couple of publications, and a few jobs under my belt—like messenger, gallery assistant, office temp. I took these jobs to make money, but there was also an aspect of penance to them. I don't know exactly for what sin I was repenting. Maybe the sin of having gone to graduate school for writing. On some level I saw these jobs as a kind of karma insurance. It was a way of testing myself: You want to be a writer? Can you handle this? How about *this*?

I wasn't so noble and pure-minded about literature that it was my only interest. I also played drums in a rock band, and I took these temporary jobs because it seemed that, on any given week, everything could change, we could sign a deal, record, go on tour. I wanted to pay the bills, take things a week at a time, and be ready for the big break. I was still high from a two-month road trip/tour the band had taken two years earlier. When that was over I only wanted to do it again. At the time it seemed inevitable, but two years later it was fading in the gauzy haze of fantasy, and I was descending into a panic.

I don't want to romanticize this panic. I think the breaking wave of the present tense is always accompanied by a whitecap of panic, as true of the moment of this writing as it was then, when I was looking for a job to pay the rent and wondering what the hell was going to happen next with everything that was important to me.

★ ★ ★

I GOT the job, in spite of being Jewish. Besides being the truth, this seemed to be the expedient answer when applying for a job at a kosher bagel factory, but it turned out that it was a minor liability. Mr. H was worried I might demand to be let off on each and every one of the many holidays—apparently some long-ago employee had given him all kinds of headaches on this matter.

My job didn't have a title, but I knew right away that it was special. I was to be in charge of inventory, which seemed a position of considerable gravity, as it included all sorts of items out of which the bagels were made (poppy seeds, raisins, sesame seeds, sourdough, salt, sugar), and I was to be paid ten dollars an hour, which I intuited was at the very high end of the pay scale at H&H. I was also to function as a kind of right-hand man to Mr. H, which meant, among other things, that I had to arrive at eight in the morning and call a series of automated voice-mail systems belonging to several different banks, get that day's balance on several different accounts, and write it all out for him so it was there as soon as he sat down at his desk at nine.

My immediate superior was a young man named Rick, a lapsed classical trumpet player from Buffalo, whose blond hair was cut Marine-short and whose glasses had small round rims that made him seem efficient and fastidious. His career had ground to a halt several years earlier when he stood backstage at a recital and found that he was incapable of going onstage. Rick had been at the bagel factory for three years and was in the midst of an extremely gradual exit. He had commenced exiting, as far as I could tell, almost as soon as he got there, and it seemed possible the process still had another year or so left in it.

Rick showed me around the ground floor, where the bagel-making took place, and the downstairs, a dungeonlike space illuminated by bare lightbulbs dangling from the ceiling. There was one long hallway, which led to a series of crevices that were used for storage, for locker rooms, for the mechanic's room.

Descending the stairs from the ground floor to the basement felt like entering another world. Each stair had a rounded edge, worn down from years of use. At the bottom of the stairs was a long passageway where one was immediately in full view of Mr. H sitting behind his desk, way at the other end. The first time I went down those stairs, I was brought up short by a very peculiar image: a pipe leading straight down from the ceiling spewing water into a white porcelain sink. The water splashed into the sink, careened around the white porcelain, and disappeared down the drain.

"What the hell is that?" I asked Rick.

"It's water from the oven, to cool the engines. It just pours down twenty-four hours a day, seven days a week. It never stops." This was a metaphor. For something. I hoped not for my time at H&H bagels.

RICK taught me the ropes.

Concerning perks: All the bagels you want, for free.

Concerning theft: You cannot steal money, but you can steal food (tuna fish, lox, orange juice, soda, ice cream). It was tacitly acceptable for us—the exalted, white, downstairs-dwelling,

Mr. H's right-hand men—to do it, but the Puerto Ricans who worked upstairs were strictly forbidden, so as a matter of courtesy we should make a point of being surreptitious.

Concerning Mr. H: Sporadically bighearted but for the most part a hard-ass in the mold of a boss who has worked his way up from the bottom. He was a Vietnam vet. A Puerto Rican from the Bronx, the youngest of eight kids, he had converted to Judaism when he got married. Some of his brothers and other relatives peppered the staff, but they got no preferential treatment, no extra pay. His oldest brother arrived at the factory in the small hours to load his truck with bagels for his delivery route. Mr. H himself had started out as a driver for the previous owners of the bakery.

There was a certain artistic quality to the precise movements of the bakers upstairs, the way they pushed slats of "doughs" into the ever-rotating carousel inside the ovens, and then flipped them, and then later removed them, but Rick assured me that Mr. H was the best, fastest, most dexterous baker at H&H and that he had once stayed up for twenty-four hours helping bake a special order, which he then single-handedly drove down to Philadelphia on no sleep.

DAYS turned into weeks. I could feel myself falling, gleefully falling into H&H Bagels, into its reality, reveling in the sheer *physicality* involved in making such a delightfully tangible thing, the sensuous, arduous, choreographed world of the bagel factory.

And nothing entranced me more than the huge, ancient ledger book in which all the inventory details were recorded, a book that would come to dominate my days, and eventually my nights as well.

When I saw that huge, decrepit, almost biblical-looking ledger book in Rick's hands, filled with tiny numerical entries, my heart leapt with recognition.

The ledger book became my domain. I studied it. In the mornings I wandered around the factory with the thing open in my arms, a pencil behind my ear, counting. All around me was the chaos of the men in white uniforms making bagels—the roar of the oven and, at the other end of the floor, the dough mixer, a hilarious machine into which huge globs of dough were fed and which then spat out measured dough sausages. A conveyor belt took them to another machine, which grabbed these dough sausages, rolled them into a loop, and dropped the loops onto another conveyor belt. A team of men stood at the end of the conveyor belt and, with expertly Chaplinesque efficiency, plucked them off one at a time and placed them on wooden platters.

Other men took the platters to a boiling cauldron and dumped the dough loops in. Still other men fished them out with a wire scoop the size of a shovel. They flung the dough loops down a moist steel gully, a bit like shuffleboard, where another crew took the boiled rings and placed them on wooden slats. Then another group of men took the slats and expertly shoved them into the oven, which had within it a continuously rotating carousel, onto which slats were pushed or flipped, and from which bagels were removed and dumped into large wire bins. The bins were then placed next to an open side door, where a huge industrial fan blew on them to cool them off.

Thus: the bagel smell on Broadway.

I counted the fifty-pound bags of poppy seeds, sesame seeds, caraway seeds, sourdough, pretzel salt, and regular salt. I counted boxes of cinnamon and raisins. I counted the number of whitefish salads, the kippered salmon salads, the tuna fish salads, and the jars of pickled herring. I counted the number of sliced lox packages, nova packages, and the whole whitefish (complete with their head, and the one dead golden eye that stared at me while I counted).

I counted the Tropicana orange juice (Original, Homestyle, Grove) and the grapefruit juice and the sodas. I counted the frozen fruits and Häagen-Dazs in the freezer up front. I counted the number of mop heads, broom handles, Brillo pad boxes, and Ajax. I counted coffee cup lids, coffee cups, and the little plastic sticks people use to stir their coffee (a thousand to a box). I counted plastic forks and spoons and knives. I counted napkins, paper towels, and rolls of toilet paper. I counted the number of white paper bags, the ones that held two bagels and the ones that held four, and six, and a dozen (plus the free extra one). I put on a coat and a scarf and a hat and entered the walk-in freezer, which held a galaxy of cream cheese products so diverse my mind reeled. I searched out the smallest, most minute things and counted them, entered the current number in the ledger, and later compared the current number to the one a few days ago to determine our rate of use and to figure out how much more to order. These long periods of contemplating the ledger book were probably the closest I've ever come to Talmudic study.

And then there was the brown sugar. Right in the middle of the bakery, like a huge chimney rising from the floor behind the cashiers, was a huge stack of fifty-pound bags of brown sugar. It sat there like a monument to its own importance.

The recipe for H&H bagels is, Mr. H informed me with a wink, top secret. But I feel, given the size and visibility of this sugar monument, that I am not betraying any trust in saying that each and every one of the bagels made there has a dollop (a pinch? a smidgen? a teaspoon?) of brown sugar in it. Twice a week a truck arrived and workers rebuilt that four-sided column of sugar from its diminished status to a magnificent, proud height. When the sugar stack was low, I felt a pang of fear in my heart; after a delivery, I could stare at it for ten straight minutes and feel all was well with the world.

DOWNSTAIRS, in a small crevice off to the side of the main office, was a row of desks. I was given one. To my left was Jay, who had been hired the same day as me. He was a slightly built Hispanic man with a thin and neatly groomed mustache, and for the first few days he arrived at work in a long black leather coat, black pants, pointy black cowboy boots, and a huge black cowboy hat. He played trombone in a Latin band that performed regularly at S.O.B.'s and other dance halls around the city. I respected his outfits. They obviously meant a lot to him. He came all the way down from the Bronx, first on a bus and then by subway, and though he spent his days hunched next to me making calls to various delis and grocery stores around the city asking after unpaid bills, he seemed intent on retaining his image as a star trombonist.

But after the first week he started showing up in sweatpants and sweatshirts. It was not a question of self-esteem, but rather of flour.

Behind us, a few feet away, was a huge flour silo. Twice a week fifty thousand pounds of flour was pumped into it from a truck that drove down from somewhere in Pennsylvania, and several times a day an engine revved up to pump flour upstairs to the dough-mixing machine. The pipes leading upstairs often sprang a leak and a fine mist of flour would fill the air. Sometimes it was so fine we would work through it, and after half an hour all of us would be very lightly frosted, as though we'd all gone a little gray. Sometimes the leaks would be more serious, and we would suddenly be engulfed in a blizzard.

Jay's outfits were getting killed. And so he gave up wearing them and surrendered his identity, during that eight-hour stretch, to being an accounts receivable guy at a bagel factory.

The flour storms did not deter Shirley, who sat to my right. She arrived at work dressed as though this were a brief stopover on her way to a shopping spree at Bergdorf Goodman. She was from one of the Caribbean Islands, had dark black skin, was very pretty, and conducted herself in a regal, aristocratic manner as though her presence at H&H were one of her good works. In fact she was putting herself through business school, which she attended at night.

Shirley handled shipping, and one of my first delinquent acts was to start picking up Shirley's line and trying to engage whomever was on it in conversation. As it was early September, I encountered a large number of mothers who were shipping bagels off to their sons and daughters who had just started college. These mothers were, on the whole, extremely willing to discuss their children.

"Bucknell?" I would say. "Really? How interesting. And what do you think your daughter might major in?" And then I'd get a whole biography. But the most eager conversationalists were those New York expatriates who for whatever reason had moved away from the big city for more pastoral environs, but who were occasionally seized with longing for the old country, which manifested itself in the need for good bagels. "The bagels out here are terrible!" they would say, speaking (rather freely, because it was an 800 number) from Salt Lake City, Atlanta, or Portland. And it was amazing, even alarming, how willing these people were to take the next step and enter into a mild confessional about how much they missed New York, and all the ways their new home was disappointing them, as though to say it to someone who was actually physically on Broadway that very second would connect them more to the place they were missing.

My responsibilities were far-reaching. I drove out to the Brooklyn Navy Yard, where a huge shipment of plastic bags with the H&H logo on them had just arrived from China, and managed to get into an at once acrimonious but somehow friendly fight on the subject of Senator Al D'Amato with the religious Jew who owned the shipping firm.

A salesman from a seed company paid a visit and Mr. H summoned me to sit by his side while the salesman poured little piles of poppy and sesame seeds out on the desk. "Taste them!" he kept saying, while he talked about prices and volume and shipping schedules, and Mr. H did, nibbling the seeds with the blank, unemotive expression of a connoisseur who didn't need to act the part. I felt a surge of pride to be part of the whole operation, and was amazed at the parts of the world with which I now had contact. It seemed vital and alive in a way an office job never could. But at the same time I was worried. This bagel job wasn't what I wanted to be. But with every moment spent thinking about the pretzel salt, the coffee stirrers, and, always, the brown sugar, it became more and more what I was. In November an anthology came out with a story of mine in it, and Shakespeare & Company put it in their window up the block. I stared at it through the glass, and vaguely wondered if I should bring a copy to the office to let them know who I was. But then, they knew who I was. I was the inventory guy.

SHORTLY after I had begun working, Mr. H called me into his office and handed me a black canvas money belt. He instructed me to put it on and, seeing it was well fastened around my waist, handed me a wad of cash totaling seven thousand dollars. He instructed me to walk the six blocks down Broadway to his bank and deposit the money.

"Wear a jacket," he said, "so no one sees it."

"I don't have a jacket."

"Take mine."

I took his jacket.

All day and all night money flowed into the registers upstairs, and a good amount of time was spent counting it, storing it, and generally organizing it. The place was awash in cash, but this was the first time I had held any of it in my hand. Large sums of bills are so weird, just paper, but with personality. It was as though the green ink of the dollars had some chemical property that briefly stunned me, and for a moment I just stood there on the black and white tiles, staring abstractedly at the cash in my hand.

"Take Jay with you," he said.

"Are you worried I'll get robbed?" I said.

Mr. H gave me one of those penetrating stares through his wire-rimmed glasses. He was always in such a swirl of papers and phone cords that when he stared right at you for more than a second it seemed significant. Now it seemed clear that he had understood the true content of my question: *You don't trust me?*

"It's about insurance," he said. "My insurance says you gotta have two people if you're moving more than five thousand dollars."

Broadway was bright with sun and people. The outdoors always seemed especially great and open after a few hours in the dungeonlike confines of the basement office; walking past that porcelain sink, with its water pouring forever down, was like walking past some mythic animal guarding its gates, promising your return. Traffic careened down the avenue, and Jay and I bopped down the street with the bounce of truant schoolkids. The pouch of the money belt was nestled in that soft private place between the bottom of my stomach and my hip, a safe, comforting place. Mr. H's windbreaker fit pretty well. I wore it open.

These bank deliveries were a frequent occurrence. Sometimes I took Jay, once in a while Rick, and on occasion one of the workers upstairs. The tight bulge of the money belt under my shirt became familiar. I felt a certain honor that Mr. H trusted me with his cash. I wondered if he was tempting me. Maybe he was taunting me. Some free time on a crowded avenue with a wad of cash strapped to your gut is stimulating to the imagination. "Where do we want to go today?" I would say to myself as I hit the street, and toy with the idea all the way to the bank.

ONE day, shortly after Thanksgiving, when I had been on the job three months and the novelty was long gone, I arrived at the factory at an unusually early hour. The job's intensity had been increasing. "Don't forget about the holiday rush," Mr. H had said to me on a number of occasions. There had been a gradual increase in the general sense of frenzy; we had all the cash registers running upstairs and still the lines stretched out the door in the morning, and again during the after-work rush hour. Those lines made the place seem like a combination of a hit Broadway show and, with its worn linoleum floors on which people stood waiting for their bread, a Depression-era soup kitchen.

On that chilly November morning my thoughts occupied the increasingly rare space in my mind that was not populated by bagels. During the previous weeks I had been on a few dates with a woman I liked. In addition to all the more familiar anxieties, I was careful to monitor her for her feelings about my current job. She seemed to think my bagel career was amusing and temporary. She thought it was an interlude, a funny story in the making. I kept my panic that this was no interlude to myself. I liked her attitude. And I liked her. And she liked me. And on the morning in question, I had woken up at her place.

I emerged from the subway into the cold air of Broadway in great spirits, triumphantly replaying certain moments from the night before, and looking forward to the calm stretch of time when I had the office to myself. It was early, and I bought a paper, got a cup of coffee, grabbed a bagel, and headed downstairs, where I gleefully sat down at Mr. H's desk and prepared for a pleasant half-hour interlude before everyone showed up. But first I made my bank calls. I had developed a weird attachment to the soft, tidy, mellifluous female voice on the automated account information line. I had come to look forward to starting my days with the sound of her voice. This placid image—the solitude, the breakfast, my paper spread out on Mr. H's desk—was so fixed in my imagination that I burrowed toward it single-mindedly, not pausing for my customary glance around the bakery floor to make sure all was well.

And so I had barely flattened the paper on the desk and taken a sip of coffee when Alberto, the night foreman who was just now coming to the end of his eight-hour shift, entered the room and, with the grave manner of a sergeant reporting bad news to an officer, removed the pointed white paper cap he and everyone else upstairs wore. He stared at me with his black eyes, which were always touched with a hint of violence.

"We're out of sugar," Alberto said.

He had worked as the night foreman for ten years and earned only a few cents an hour more than I. Like most of the workers upstairs, he was Puerto Rican. He understood my role at the company, my prerogatives and my perks. There was no sympathy in his eyes. I stared at them anyway.

"We ran out around five o'clock in the morning," he said. "I've had thirty guys sitting on their asses for two and a half hours." He ran a hand slowly over his slicked-back hair, as though this bit of information might have, in the very telling, unsettled it, put his paper cap back on, and went back upstairs.

I had underestimated the holiday rush. The ever-fluctuating but always formidable pillar of brown sugar had been vanquished.

I went into the blankly efficient mode of the deeply freaked out. I called my sugar supplier and begged him to let me have some of the inventory that he had already loaded onto a truck headed for other destinations. Then, having been promised enough to get me through the day, I sank into a numb state of dread. I felt a little like someone who had borrowed his father's car, driven around like a big shot for a while, and then crashed it. I monitored the approach of Mr. H like someone watching a hurricane on a weather monitor. I could only watch the clouds gather and hope the storm was brief.

The gale was of hurricane force. Mr. H just happened to arrive a bit late that day, so it took place in view of the whole office. Mr. H was a hands-on manager. Every one of the myr-iad details concerning the production and shipping and sell-ing of his bagels was in his head—he delegated with reluctance. And now his worst fears had come true. He came barreling down that narrow alley that funneled right into the black-and-white-tiled room, his face a scrunched-up ball of red. This collapsed-in-rage face was an expression I recog-nized from my old basketball coach. By now Mr. H would have passed the empty platter where the sugar stack normally rose, he would have seen the idle workers sitting around, the machines all still. He started screaming at a distance of twenty feet. And as he screamed and yelled at me and waved his arms around—all this with his coat still on, his paper still in his hand, his scarf still wrapped around his neck—I could

see in his angry features another, quieter and more complicated exasperation: One day I come in twenty minutes late
and everything falls apart! he seemed to be thinking. He had
a family, but his business was his baby. It consumed him even
as it fed him.

He raged on until I pointed out that it was Tuesday. Tuesday
was the day I did a massive inventory of the cream cheeses, and
the order had to be in by ten-thirty. I put on my coat, my scarf,
my gloves, and retreated into the cold humming silence of the
old walk-in freezer, the ledger book open in my arms, and
began the process of counting, and penance.

I overcompensated, and placed a mammoth sugar order.
The next morning a crew of men carried it in from the truck
on their shoulders. They made the stack in its customary place.
It rose up like a very narrow log cabin, but there were still more
bags. They found a place for them in the stairway. But there
were still more bags. By the time they were done, the entire factory looked like a World War I trench. A bunker. The staircase,
the hallways downstairs, every available space was lined with
fifty-pound bags of brown sugar, as though we were sandbag-
ging a river that threatened to flood. Getting to work downstairs meant that everyone now had to turn their shoulders
sideways so as to fit through what little space remained. The
complaints were endless, though curiously the only person
who did not chastise me was Mr. H himself. His was a tunnel
vision, and I suspected that the space his body was now com-
pelled to move through was no larger than the space through
which his mind always moved, and so he hardly noticed it. All
he registered was that we had enough sugar; and perhaps he
wanted to give me a break. I was a quantity to be burned

through fast and then replaced; just as a basketball coach will drive his team hard at the start of the season and soften up toward the end, I think Mr. H was instinctively letting up on me in preparation for my departure.

FOLLOWING the sugar disaster, I redoubled my efforts to get out of the bagel factory. I had been focusing my moneymaking energies in what was meant to be my profession—writing. I would make numerous phone calls from my desk to magazine editors, trying to scrounge up some freelance work. There were two obstacles to success in this endeavor. One was that other than a short story that I had published in *The New Yorker*, I had very little in the way of credentials.

The other problem was the dough mixer. With some regularity the enormous engine would switch on, making a sound similar in texture and volume to a big airplane getting ready to take off. This tended to complicate my phone conversations with editors.

"What's that?" they would say when the engine kicked in. I'm at the airport? I'm at the heliport? I'm at the hairdresser's?

"I'm at work," I would reply, and usually, thinking that offense is better than defense, I would add, "I'm working at a bagel factory."

"Oh, how wonderful!" was a common reply.

At last I pulled my ace in the hole—I called my editor at *The New Yorker*. The flour silo's engine did not turn on. The call was brief. I told him about the bagel factory. He didn't seem to think it was such a bad thing. He was perilously close to joining the ranks of the "Oh, how wonderfuls!" I asked if the magazine needed someone to lick stamps or sweep the floor. He said they had those bases covered. He suggested that perhaps I could do a piece of nonfiction, something short, and asked if I had any ideas.

I blurted out the name of Esteban Vicente, an old painter with whom I was acquainted, who was having a ninetieth birthday coming up and an exhibit to go along with it. Vicente had once shared a studio with de Kooning and had become famous along with Jackson Pollock and all the other New York School painters, but his star had waned. Now he was obscure. But he had continued to paint, oblivious to his professional fluctuations, or at least not unmoored by them, and was now having something of a revival.

It was agreed that I would write a very short profile—more like a long blurb—to go along with a full-page reproduction of one of his paintings.

SUDDENLY Esteban Vicente became the focus of my existence, along with Euro-Disney, who had placed a mammoth order for our bagels. Every day for a week I drove a truck out to a warehouse in a desolate section of Long Island City. The truck was packed to the brim with boxes of bagels, each about fifteen pounds. I would throw each box into the arms of a scrawny black kid who stood on the loading dock and stacked them on a platter, which then was wrapped in a giant roll of Saran Wrap and finally driven by forklift into a monstrous freezer, from which they would be shipped to France for the consumption of European people looking at Mickey Mouse and Goofy. It was arduous physical labor. The boxes got heavier throughout the afternoon. My back was a mess. The skinny guy caught each one into his chest. We didn't have the energy to talk. I kept thinking: I'm killing myself for Euro-Disney!

I went to Vicente's studio on West Forty-second Street to interview him. We sat and talked for a long time—I had called in sick, not entirely a lie because my back could not take another day of throwing boxes—and the longer I talked, the more I began to feel that it was a strange coincidence that I should be coming to know this man at this particular time.

There was something wonderfully impervious about him, and resilient. He had a self-worth that in someone else could become vanity, but vanity is always defining itself against the appreciation of others. The only compass Vicente was watching was his own. Vicente was an education in how much single-mindedness is necessary if you want to survive as an artist.

"Like every human being, I want to be loved, but I want to be loved on my own terms," he said. "No one told me to be a painter—it's my responsibility. Artists have a purpose in life, but you must make the effort. Through effort you have joy."

These rather grand emotions did not, however, mitigate my rather craven ambitions to get my piece in print, to get paid, to see my name published somewhere besides an H&H paycheck, and I faxed the article from the bagel factory in the spirit of someone buying a lottery ticket. I had worked on it all night. After I sent it in I put in a good day's work, buoyed by the thought that my days at H&H were numbered. I returned home that night ready to submerge myself in bed and sleep, but not before, just on cue, as my eyes closed heavily, the phone rang—it was my editor, who in his typical measured tones told me, "We liked the piece." He said he would call me later in the week. I slept deeply.

THE next day was Tuesday, cream cheese day, and I went about my duties in the walk-in freezer in a state of elation. Wednesday went by quickly. Thursday, disaster struck. I received a call from my editor saying that there was a problem with the art department. Apparently someone somewhere had raised an objection to reprinting a full page of abstract art. Vicente had been asked for a self-portrait.

The man had been an abstract painter for over forty years, and this after a very considered decision to stop painting and exhibiting figurative work. I didn't think he was a prime candidate for a self-portrait. I amused myself with a mock speech I could deliver to him about how, maybe just a few dots with a mouth beneath it, it would mean so much to . . . me! To everyone! Hey, it's exposure! But if there was ever a nonpragmatist, it was Vicente. He didn't give a damn about exposure, and for this I admired him.

I drove my truck full of bagels out to Long Island City, parked it on a side street, and crawled back to lay among the boxes, warm and fragrant (they were all sesame bagels that day). I fell asleep. By now my job had thoroughly infiltrated my dreams: Every other night I had anxiety dreams about running out of whitefish salad. I had another anxiety dream amid the boxes of bagels. I dreamed that I slept in a bagel submarine that never came up for air. I opened my eyes, and the dream continued. This was my life. The fact that it was this beautiful moment of comfort and peace—all those boxes of bread around me muffling the outside world, warming me, the consoling smell—just made it more complicated. Vicente, I knew then, would never do a self-portrait.

LATER that day I returned from the Euro-Disney job and called my answering machine. We were in the midst of one of the minor flour leaks, and I sat being slowly covered in white powder. I got a message saying that Esteban Vicente had done a self-portrait. I leapt to my feet. I floated through the flour-saturated air. I ran my hands through huge vats of poppy seeds and watched them pour through my fingers as though they were treasure. I went to an out-of-the-way crevice and threw punches at a sack of sourdough like it was a heavy bag, ducking and weaving, ready for my shot at the championship. I was outrageously happy! The piece was on! Vicente would do the self-portrait!

But gradually this elation gave way to something else. How could Vicente agree to such a thing? My elation turned to a kind of mild, sour grief. Had the voice of commerce lulled his artistic integrity? Had he been bullied into doing something for pragmatic reasons? Did he whip off lots of self-portraits all the time and not tell anyone?

And as I contemplated this, I came to realize that intertwined with all my admiration for the man was a little strand of resentment. This is the weird thing that often accompanies one's appraisal of the virtuous—I had regarded his integrity ever so slightly as a reproach. But now, as I considered that it might have faltered, I missed it. I was rooting for it and lamenting it. As much as I wanted the piece to run, I did not want Esteban Vicente to sell out.

The next day, clutching the phone as the flour silo roared in the background, I was told that Esteban had in fact handed in the self-portrait. The magazine had the self-portrait. It was a . . .

The roar of the flour silo drowned out the words. I waited twenty seconds and asked the person at the other end of the line to repeat herself. "The self-portrait was a splotch of red," she said.

The piece was killed. But my seven hundred words landed on the magazine's new editor-in-chief's desk entirely by accident, and found there a receptive audience. The piece was going to run, after all, and she wanted to meet me.

I LASTED at H&H through the New Year. Other than a small pretzel-salt crisis there were no major mishaps. In late January I gave Mr. H my notice. He responded coolly to this, but did not seem too upset.

Later that afternoon he had a heart attack. I helped carry him up the stairs, still sitting in his chair, past the porcelain sink into which the endless waterfall poured. The place was in an uproar as we watched the paramedics put an oxygen mask on his face. Among the white-suited workers upstairs, the men Mr. H ruled with a strong hand (primarily by paying them little more than minimum wage, not giving them any vacation time until they worked there nine months, and not allowing so much as the scent of a union to enter the floor), there was a surge of genuine grief. Everyone spilled out of the side entrance to watch silently as the paramedics loaded him into the ambulance. They all took off their hats.

Downstairs, we had to deal with the fact that, at the time he had the heart attack, Mr. H was counting out a huge sum of cash, which lay untended on his desk. About five different people volunteered to be responsible for it. I prevailed. In my dreamy fantasies about theft and revenge I could not have conjured a more enticing scenario. But I counted the money out scrupulously, totaled it, and put it back in a white paper bag (the size for a dozen bagels) as was the custom, and dropped it in the ancient black safe in the corner.

I WATCHED my replacement be interviewed. He had graduated from Deerfield, then Dartmouth. He was an aspiring actor. I showed him around the place, presented him with the ledger book, and informed him that when Mr. H asked him to read something, it didn't mean his expert opinion was being asked, you were just supposed to paraphrase. The rest was up to him to figure out.

Shortly before my last day, I found myself standing in the walk-in freezer wearing a suit. I had an appointment with *The New Yorker*'s editor-in-chief that morning, and I was racing through the cream cheese inventory so as to be on time. I stood in the walk-in freezer and slowly counted, enjoying the ritual, the strange environment, the privacy. As always the heavy door to the freezer was slightly ajar. And then, for the first time since I had been working there, someone bumped the door, and the ancient metal bolt clicked shut. I carefully put the ledger book on some boxes of olive and pimiento cream cheese and commenced to bang hysterically on the inside of that door, screaming at the top of my lungs to be let out. I was screaming in fear—that I would miss my appointment, that my big chance would be squandered because I was locked in the cream cheese freezer—but I was also laughing. The bagel factory was clutching me for one last moment in its absurd embrace. And when the door was pulled open at last and I was free to rise up out of that place forever, I felt a tiny pang of sorrow to have been released so soon.

THE PROBLEM WITH T-SHIRTS

★

26 years old

THE OTHER DAY I WENT TO A PARTY WEARING AN OLD T-shirt to which I had grown attached. You should never wear a beloved item of clothing out in public, if that item of clothing happens to be a T-shirt. This shirt had existed in a state of semiretirement for a while on account of its age, but I was wearing it to amuse a friend, who had once edited a magazine whose name was now on my chest. The magazine had lasted a year. The T-shirt had outlasted it by more than a decade.

Halfway through the party someone said, "What's up with all the holes?" She flicked her hand at one of them, somewhere below the chest. Was this a hostile gesture? Flirtatious? Was she thinking about another friend of mine, who had strung her along for such a long time and then announced that he was engaged to someone else?

I don't know. I don't think she intended to rip the shirt off my back, but that was what happened. The whole shirt rolled itself up like a window shade and more or less vanished, leaving the collar around my neck and some material hanging on my back. I changed into another shirt and brought the T-shirt home. It was beyond repair, more of a shroud than a shirt, but it took a few weeks of moving it around the house from one place to another before I realized I had to finally throw it out. I had this realization, and then put the shroud back in a drawer, where it hung around for another year or so before I came to my senses and got rid of it.

THERE are those for whom a T-shirt is just another name for an undershirt, the sort of thing that never sees the light of day. But for a lot of others, myself included, T-shirts often are a staple.

Like most people, my T-shirt collection has developed in a haphazard manner—a free one here, an impulse buy there. Even at the time of their acquisition, they are negligible possessions, and get treated as such. No other item of clothing is valued less than T-shirts, in spite of the fact that a T-shirt single-handedly turns its wearer into a walking billboard (even the plain white ones carry a kind of James Dean circa *Rebel Without a Cause* message). They are often drenched in sweat during some strenuous physical exercise, or spattered with bits of food, since the state of hyperawareness that exists while eating in a nice dress shirt is absent while eating in a T-shirt, which of course is part of its appeal. Then they get crumpled up and thrown in a corner or rudely stuffed in a hamper.

Socks admittedly give it competition in the No Respect category, but sock enthusiasts will point out that socks are capable of levels of style and elegance that a T-shirt could never attain. The other logical competition for lowest spot on the wardrobe totem pole would be underwear, but we live in the age of underwear—Victoria's Secret has built an Empire of Underwear. Entire museum exhibitions are dedicated to it, and walking around New York these days, one is surrounded by a kaleidoscope of underwear imagery: on buses, on billboards, and on people.

Now and then a T-shirt fad will pop up, but they're never very convincing. Once there was "Frankie Says Relax," then the Phillies Blunt logo, then old concert T-shirts from dinosaur rock bands, and the innocent high school sports T-shirts from small-town America.

I've always preferred more eclectic T-shirts, such as the one that promotes a publication called *Pain Digest.* It got sent to me by a friend who works in the pharmaceuticals industry. The logo sprawls across the chest, big white letters against dark blue, and the phrase "Advanced Literature for Pain" runs across the back. This item always draws out a few curious stares.

T-shirts get worn all year, but warm weather is their prime time. Recently, with the arrival of T-shirt weather, I found myself in a contemplative mood, staring into a drawer devoted exclusively to T-shirts. I had just done the wash, and they lay in two neat square piles, like a multicolored layer cake. Some were fairly new, while others nearly twenty years old. Each of the older ones had been acquired during a long-departed era. They were like souvenirs from a trip I'd once taken. I reached into the pile and felt fabric as soft as cashmere and as cool and smooth as silk.

And here is the real problem with T-shirts: They improve with age, getting better and better, until one day they disappear. Their finest moment is their grand finale. This is true of shoes and jeans, too, but shoes can always be resoled and jeans can be patched, and both, when all is finally lost, still have a physical presence, a weight you can feel on your hand. But T-shirts will just keep getting thinner and finer until they're gone. One moment it is perfect, and then a tiny hole appears, and then another; a tear along the seam might develop, and one day you reach into your drawer and pull out what to the untrained eye would look like a handkerchief. Or someone touches your shirt at a party and it disappears off your back. What then?

Of course you just throw it out. But there's a catch. One doesn't have to be wildly sentimental to get attached to a T-shirt that used to belong to an old flame, or the one advertising a high school or college in faded letters, or even that ridiculous thing that one swore would never see the light of day but has taken on some importance because you were a whole other person when you first slipped it on. These objects are as evocative as snapshots. They're documents, but they can't be reproduced.

My own solution, I discovered that day, is an informal T-shirt Hall of Fame. Way down at the bottom of the drawer several T-shirts are lying in state, like antiquities. Sometimes, when I'm fumbling around for a newer model, I'll reach down into the cool darkness and brush against their fragile surfaces, waiting there like understudies for one last day in the sun.

A BIKER
IN THE
CITY

★

28 years old

FOR SOME PEOPLE, A BICYCLE IS SOMETHING TO BE taken out for a pleasant jaunt in the park on weekends, an opportunity to feel the breeze in your hair and to coast alongside novice rollerbladers whose eyes are wide with terror. Then there are the brave souls who use it to make a living, the bicycle messengers, a group I once belonged to. For others, however, myself included, a bicycle is simply the best way to get around the city, and it's the best way to see the city as well.

A bike is the best way to see the quilt of neighborhoods that meld seamlessly into one another. "Neighborhood" is not even the correct word—biking through the city is like moving through a series of moods.

And looking at people is different when you're on a bicycle. Whereas most New Yorkers shun anything more than fleeting eye contact while walking down the street, a pedestrian and bike rider can engage in the kind of languorous exchange of glances that are usually reserved for people looking at each other from opposite sides of a pane of glass. The street scenes you see are fragmented mini-movies, out of context and intriguing.

Biking in the city accentuates that most powerful of city feelings, being alone in a crowd. You are never more part of the flow of the city life than when you are getting around on your bike, and yet you are somehow above it. There have been times I thought I knew every inch of the streets of Manhattan and yet I never really set foot on any of it. Witness bikers held up at a red light. Often they will go in little circles, or do an acrobatic kind of balancing act in which they hold themselves still with their brakes, moving forward an inch here and there, just to keep balance, until the light changes and they are on their way. The point is, they don't want to put their feet on the ground. To do so would be . . . pedestrian. Biking in the city is all about momentum, flow, prerogative, and also a kind of painterly perspective.

On a bicycle you experience most acutely the surreal juxtapositions between big and small. There was a time when I was sure I could narrate every inch of certain stretches of Sixth Avenue, or upper Broadway, or Avenue A, I mean every black smudge of old gum, every pothole, every piece of gravel. When you are on your bike you look down, you look up, you see patterns. I was recently shooting down Broadway from the Upper Upper West Side, debating whether to take the gorgeous new bike highway that now runs alongside the Hudson River. I hit the fork at 107th Street—Broadway or River? City or country? Through the heart of the island, or the dreamy waterside express?

I voted for the river and took West End Avenue. There on 101st Street, and then on 100th Street, were the last two phone booths in all of New York. I swept past them in a blur, shooting downhill, but it was like a visit with friends. Getting around on a bike makes all of the city your friend and, on some unreasonable, irrational psychic level, your property. You belong to the city and the city belongs to you, and that is beautiful, except when it's not.

ONCE I was biking down Broadway toward Midtown, enjoying the burst of speed that begins with the incline at Fifty-fourth Street, when a brand-new blue sports car pulled up beside me, its multiple antennas bristling in various directions. It was a crisp bright morning, around that time of year when spring is no longer tentative and pale green fronds are sprouting all over the place, even in Midtown Manhattan. I was wearing my old bike messenger bag. I like wearing it; it testifies to my days as a serious biker. But it also puts me in my old combative mood, and so I did not take kindly to this shiny sports car a few inches from my right leg.

I was in the bicycle lane—more a formality than anything, but a comforting one—and for a moment the car was right beside me. I was about to glance into the window to see who was driving, but it suddenly jumped ahead and made a sharp left onto Forty-eighth Street, cutting me off badly and sending me into a skid. For a second I was outside the scene, watching myself from a distance as my brakes locked and the car's rear bumper brushed my leg. Then I was back in the moment, safe and undamaged, my own antenna bristling.

Common sense, civility, and sheer survival instinct should have dictated that I go on my way, but I was in the grip of something else—my old bike messenger persona, perhaps. Or maybe just spring. Or maybe I was in the grip of that chemical road rage reaction. Road rage is usually about fear. Either that or an irrational, almost impossible-to-resist temptation to see the thing literally obstructing your forward motion as representing *everything in the world that is obstructing your forward motion*. In this case it was a bit of both.

The blue car rolled to a stop at a red light down the block. I headed off after it, furious. As I approached, an ambulance came up behind me, heading east on Forty-eighth Street, on its way to or from some other catastrophe. Its sirens wailed at a volume designed to cut through the Midtown din. It was an appropriately apocalyptic soundtrack to the moment, and as I came up next to the car, shimmering in its newness, I administered a violent kick to its side. The resulting sound was similar to that of a piece of paper being crumpled up, which surprised me for some reason. There was something about the way the metal gave way so innocently that struck a chord within me. It was the exhausted capitulation of the New to the forces of Decay and Destruction, of which, at that moment, I was an agent.

I coasted past the car and turned to make a vehement and obscene gesture at the driver, who, obligingly, was already in the midst of vehemently making the same gesture at me. At this moment I glimpsed, through the glare of the windshield, what appeared to be a well-dressed man jumping up and down in his seat in a manner that reminded me, for some reason, of Evander Holyfield just after Mike Tyson bit off a piece of his ear.

It made me smile, but it also made me wish I hadn't turned to look. It's a tricky thing, this documenting of revenge, because though it satisfies the desire to see the enemy vanquished, or at least annoyed, it invariably creates a whole new problem, transforming the enemy from an abstract machine into a human being with bills and lovers and parents and so forth who looks funny jumping up and down in the front seat of his car.

The ambulance slowed beside the car. The sirens cut off and the block seemed momentarily quiet. Then a voice emanated from the ambulance, tremendously amplified, you could hear it for blocks, yet conversational in tone, almost tender. It said, "I think he damaged your car."

Damaged! What had I done? I scampered down Seventh Avenue, remorse already building within me.

I'm tempted to say that it is this fact—that the bike is the ultimate getaway vehicle—that makes bike riders so capable of violence. I know I am not alone in this sort of reaction. Seemingly mild-mannered, ecologically sensitive, kindhearted bikers can go absolutely nuts when they feel wronged. I once saw my own literary agent, who I met while riding a bike, and who is a woman who does not seem violent, rush off after a car that had brushed her in order to pound the windshield and scream at the driver. It was a shock. After she did this she turned her bike around and hastily headed in the opposite direction, unaware I happened to witness the whole thing.

Now, after the ambulance announced my crime, I went into fugitive mode and anxiously darted through the streets, calculating a route that made my victim least likely to catch up. Every police car I saw sent my heart racing. But I was safe, an anonymous vandal, vanished into a city so hospitable to that act.

Later, I decided that biking in the city entails a kind of Faustian bargain with its streets: You can float above them, see the city from the safe distance of the voyeur, but every now and then it becomes part of you.

TURTLES
IN
NEW YORK

★

28 years old

FOR A FEW WEEKS ONE SUMMER, TURTLES ENJOYED a brief vogue in New York—turtles whose shells weren't much bigger than a silver dollar were sold on street corners all over Manhattan, and people crowded around to buy them. In the midst of this turtle trend, my friend Kip moved back to New York, after two years in Los Angeles, and it was only a few days before he was swept up in the turtle craze. "I got them on the street, in Chinatown, five dollars each," he told me excitedly. "That's the great thing about New York. One minute you're walking down the street and then all of a sudden you're a turtle owner."

When Kip went to buy a habitat for his new pets, he found the store jammed with people looking at aquariums and inquiring about turtle food. "It's turtle mania. I don't understand it," the store manager said. Kip bought an aquarium, some props for inside the aquarium, including a fake plant and a brick ("to give the environment some architecture," he explained), and a supply of minnows, which functioned as scenery until the turtles ate them.

Kip, being a baseball fan and a native of Minnesota, named the two turtles Kirby Puckett and Rod Carew. For the first few weeks I heard a great deal about the charming exploits of Rod and Kirby. "It was so great," he would say; "Kirby was asleep, you know, all balled up in his little shell, just sleeping on top of the brick, and then he fell off. He just fell off the brick and floated down to the bottom, and when he landed he stuck his little head out and looked really confused." There was a great deal of speculation about Rod and Kirby's relationship. Did they get along? Who was more powerful? And most importantly, were they happy?

It was around this time that the turtles began to make the news. They had been smuggled into the city from turtle farms in such far-off places as Louisiana and Florida and were reported to carry salmonella. The ASPCA—who were being inundated with calls from new turtle owners wondering how to care for them—raided a distribution center, located in an alley behind the old police headquarters on Center Street, and confiscated over three thousand tiny turtles, whose scientific name is *Trachemys scripta elegans*. Many of the turtles, it turns out, still had a "hatching tooth" and were less than a month old. The ASPCA, along with city and federal officials—who were acting on a Food and Drug Administration policy that bans inter- or intrastate sale and distribution of turtles less than four inches in length—cracked down on the street venders and, for the moment at least, the turtle trade was eradicated.

Kip, however, was having his own, more private drama with Rod and Kirby. He had moved into a new apartment and was looking for work, without much luck. He was spending a lot of time at home. The city hummed along, impervious of his efforts to join its life. For weeks I didn't hear much about the pair until one day he said, "Rod and Kirby are starting to depress me. They paw at the glass. It's kind of disturbing. They swim right up to the glass and kind of paw at it with their little turtle hands like they want to get out. I sit here all day in my little apartment watching them in their little aquarium. I feel like I'm their jailer." Kip began to fasten to the idea that he was somehow holding the pair captive against their will.

Then one day he decided to set them free. He found a place that struck him as a good turtle habitat—the pond near the weather castle in Central Park. I met him there for the big event. He brought them in a small portable aquarium, a container with some water on the bottom. It was a brilliant autumn afternoon, a Sunday, and, by coincidence, the last day of regular-season baseball; Central Park was brimming with strollers, and a group of ducks quacked and paddled festively in the center of the pond. The world seemed huge and full of possibilities.

Rod and Kirby seemed extremely small. Kip set the aquarium down on the grass and we took a close look. Their shells were bright green and they moved around excitedly, sensing a big change. One of them came up to the plastic wall and started pawing at it. Kip was right. It was disturbing. After a few minutes Kip tipped the box on its side. There was a moment of confusion, and then the pair began to make their way forward, toward the water. Rod jumped right in and started paddling out toward the ducks in the center of the pond. Kirby was more reluctant, hesitating at the water's edge for a minute before plopping in. He moved around in the shallows while Rod swam farther and farther away, a tiny speck of animated green just beneath the water's surface.

"I wonder if they'll stay friends," said Kip.

ABOUT five years after this scene, I was brought up short by a sign in front of this pond. It had been called Belvedere Lake. Now it was called Turtle Pond. It turns out the name was changed because the place had become a Mecca for disaffected turtle owners. They came here from all over the city to set them free. I don't know if this means that Rod and Kirby encountered some other confused members of their tribe—maybe they made *new* friends—but it took me aback to think that, minutes or hours after Kip and I had walked away from our solemn mission, another pair stepped up to the edge of the pond with their plastic aquarium and, after a thoughtful moment, delicately tipped it on its side.

THE
BREAKUP

32 years old

ROUTE 1 IS A LONG THIN ROAD THAT CONNECTS THE Florida Keys with the mainland of Florida. The little islands are like jewels on a necklace and the highway is the string that holds them all together. Driving down Route 1 on a still, sunny day, you feel like you are on a precarious high wire suspended over a vast net of light blue ocean. It feels like paradise, though there are warnings that life isn't always so calm. All along Route 1 are little blue signs: "Hurricane Evacuation Route."

One sunny afternoon you might have been driving down that road and seen a particular kind of tempest, immediately recognizable to anyone who is now—or has ever been—part of a couple.

You are on one of the sparsely populated Keys,

hardly a tiki hut or souvenir stand in sight. A car is pulled off to the side of the road. The hood isn't up; there is no engine trouble. No one is taking a pee in the bushes or rearranging stuff in the trunk. This is another kind of trouble—a man and woman are walking in opposite directions away from the car.

I'VE always been amazed at the different tactics in fights that occur between lovers, as opposed to two guys having it out. Of course couples get violent, but the whole mechanism of anger is different.

Fights between two men tend to involve two bodies coming together. Fights between a man and woman, on the other hand, quite often involve two bodies moving apart. Fights between men start with a lot of aggressive shouting; the business of actually throwing a punch is often weirdly silent. All the energy is, if only for a second, rerouted into the physical act of violence. Romantic fights, on the other hand, often begin with taunts of silence; talking, or shouting, is a sign that things are taking their course.

Men start hot and cool off. Men and women, when they fight, start cold, with a rage more freezing than dry ice, and then finally the earth splits open and out pour tears, recriminations, apologies, confessions as hot as molten lava.

THERE is only one lane in each direction on Route 1. The speed limit is fifty miles an hour. Everyone is driving along staring at the scenery. And here is a scene: a car pulled off to the side of the road, a woman walking away from it in one direction, a man walking away in the other. Their footsteps draw two pencil lines in the dry pale grass, a diagram of separation.

Then the man stops, turns around, starts walking back to the car, then passes it; he breaks into a trot, then a run, and catches up to the woman. She keeps walking. He reaches for her elbow. Even at fifty miles an hour you would have recognized that moment, a universal moment in the choreography of fights between men and women, when the man reaches for the woman's elbow and she, in fury, yanks it away. That gesture says: Get off of me. It says: Leave me alone. And it says, more than anything: I can't believe that of all the men in the world it's you who I'm stuck with by the side of the road.

She swerves right, into a break in the dense roadside foliage, and a little path appears. Now you enter another dimension in which a gemlike perfection of design descends onto the situation—everything falls into place and makes a weird, horrible kind of sense.

So of course the narrow path quickly leads to a clearing and suddenly it's quiet. The man and the woman are standing, rather incongruously, amid a sea of old lobster traps stacked in towering ramshackle piles, a graveyard of boxy rectangles of bleached wood sitting in sunny retirement. The sun beats down brightly, a reminder of happier moments at Key West.

The roadside show is now over, and in the privacy of that enclave, amid the old wooden boxes that were once full of life (literally) but are now relics, all hell breaks loose. The woman is furious, hysterical, grieving, crying, unforgiving. About what? That day's original sin is long out of sight, forgotten, a tiny banana peel that led to a slip that led to a swerve, and shortly a world war has broken out that is out of proportion with its origins. She's lashing out violently, but the object of her wrath—to his amazement and horror—is herself. She bangs herself on her head. Hard blows to the head. Self-inflicted wounds. The man watches this for a moment in shock and then begins gushing apologies. He reaches for her wrists to stop her. He grovels. He begs.

"Please," he says.

She screams at him to leave her alone.

"I hate . . ." she begins.

She's crying and screaming and hitting herself. The blows land on him by accident when he tries to get in her way.

"I hate myself for loving you," she blurts out.

Holy shit! thinks the man. She's quoting Joan Jett! Does she know that?

Such are the internal monologues of a man standing amid a ruin of old lobster traps behind the roadside brush off Route 1, as his girlfriend of two years beats herself and has a nervous breakdown because their relationship is clearly going down the tubes for the simple reason that he doesn't love her, or love her enough to marry her. Which is not really a simple reason.

The banana peel, the straw that broke the camel's back, the little pebble that led to this avalanche, is sufficiently absurd that it bears reporting. What happened was that I, the man in this scene, having promised not to, had smoked some pot. A crime of high school, back for an encore. I had taken a quick hit under a particularly extravagant blooming tree down the street from the public library in Key West. Our drive down had been a debauch, mutually undertaken, various powders and liquids, but at some point we decided to clean up. And then I had made a solo expedition, a brief reconnaissance mission behind the lines, a visit to the land of the fucked-up. Which was worse, the doing it or the sneaking it? What did it matter? The technicalities, the little points of procedure, the litigious evasions, the tap dance of excuses—they never hold up in places like that clearing, where the truth comes out and the judgment is summary.

IT'S so odd to look back on a relationship long after its conclusion and see it from up above, as one might view a valley and the surrounding mountains from a small plane. All those incredibly important seconds that composed your life together are like pine needles on the ground, invisible beneath the trees. You see it drifting away from you down below, as though in a dream. Maybe you wanted to leave that land, or maybe you were exiled, but either way, I think, you look back with a mixture of amazement and horror—you lived there, and now you're gone.

AT the same time, you see the landscape's structure and logic with a clarity you never did when you were living in it. Jill and I had been going out for two years. Courage in relationships is often seen in terms of having the strength to walk away from a bad situation. But it's much harder to walk away from a good situation, one in which the current moment is sweet, and yet you never let go of the feeling that this is just a visit, temporary. Courage is being willing to be the bad guy, as opposed to the victim. After a year or so, in your thirties as I was, or approaching it, as Jill was, you simply have to own up to your ambivalence and raise the stakes on the matter. At a certain point, you can't think of ambivalence as being some mysterious shackle on love; you have to acknowledge that the nature of your love isn't strong enough to overcome your ambivalence. Whose fault is that? It doesn't matter. The fault—my fault, in this case—is not coming clean. Why—besides the sheer inconvenience—don't people come clean? Maybe you just think you're in love because it's a necessary myth. If you're not, what the hell are you doing here, other than being an example of how being comfortable is not sufficient? Being comfortable is not enough! Comfort, as a relationship's greatest virtue, eventually becomes uncomfortable. You end up in a thorny grove surrounded by old lobster traps.

The scene among the old lobster traps was not the very end. In fact the next days were strangely clear and beautiful, the serene crisp calm after the storm. Driving with Jill was always one of the great pleasures, and we still had to get all the way back to New York from the southernmost point in the United States.

THE idea for a trip occurred to us during those first insufferable days of March, when one waits for spring with all the patience of a commuter waiting for a long-delayed bus.

Both she and I had hit a few exasperating bumps in our work and we needed to get away from everything, including ourselves. This is not the same as getting away from each other. I could get away from me, she could get away from her, and we could then romp across the country like convicts escaped from the shackles of our own lives.

We'd taken road trips like this before. A year earlier, we'd taken a trip through the South in her old college car when we had been together a year. Even then, certain nagging questions about where we were going were starting to surface like alligators in a pond. I could see just their eyes, peering above the surface and posing the question, "What are you going to do next?" The eyes looked innocent, but I knew that barely submerged, just out of sight, was a vicious set of teeth that was going to eat me alive. This, for some reason, was what I thought of marriage. Perhaps those teeth are too Freudian an image. Maybe it was more like that feeling one sometimes has swimming in the ocean, when you don't want your toes to go all the way down to where it is cold and you can't see, so you keep yourself as close to the surface as you can. A road trip is like that. It's lateral motion, skimming the surface.

This time her father was lending us a Jeep Cherokee. He'd had the tires checked before we left. I respected the tenderness of this gesture, even as I knew we would more or less nullify all safety concerns with whatever recreational drugs we were bringing along. I was glad for the sturdy vehicle, but it also seemed confining. Its reliability was annoying. I resisted this bland vehicle and what it stood for in my life. Looking back, I think the brave thing to do would have been to acknowledge that feeling and end the whole thing right there. Instead I took the Jeep, and its owner's daughter, for a ride.

WE headed off early one Sunday morning. The car was loaded with a couple bags of clothes, a lot of music for the stereo, a basketball, and other supplies.

It was a cold sunny morning. The streets of Manhattan were deserted and beautiful in that way that things are when you are about to leave them. We got in the car and started to drive.

"I want to get a coffee and a muffin," I said.

"Don't," she said. "You'll get crumbs all over the car."

"Oh, come on," I said. Three blocks after we started, I pulled over at a familiar breakfast place. I got coffee and a muffin.

I took a bite and drove. I took a sip. I took a bite. There were crumbs on my lap. I pulled over. We were on a completely empty street near the Holland Tunnel. I chucked the muffin. The coffee I poured into the gutter after a last sip. It was a cold morning, and I remember the brown liquid steaming. Throwing away the coffee and the muffin was like a baptism in reverse. A symbol of all my habits, bad and otherwise, that I was leaving behind in New York.

OUR first day of driving stretched late into the night. We were adamant about getting far away from anywhere familiar. Somewhere in North Carolina all signs of civilization vanished. The blackness extended for miles. Finally we came upon a Comfort Inn in Cape Hatteras. Our location in the world was a mystery to everyone but ourselves. We were off the grid.

The next morning we both stirred awake at an unusually early hour. The blinds were open and we stepped over to the window to see the Atlantic Ocean, a vast metallic blue, lapping calmly against the shore. Just below us was an empty swimming pool surrounded by a wooden patio on which beach chairs, pool toys, and umbrellas sat in a mild state of disarray, as though a scene of summer frolic had been suddenly abandoned months ago and no one had been back since. Now it awaited the animating touch of spring to bring it all back to life. The combination of the abandoned pool and the empty sea made us feel like the last people on earth. We fell back onto the beautiful bed with its clean, white, anonymous sheets.

"TO any other type of tourist accommodation I soon grew to prefer the functional motel—clean, neat, safe nooks, ideal places for sleep, arguments, reconciliation, insatiable illicit love."

So begins part two of Vladimir Nabokov's, *Lolita*.

There is something about a motel that makes love seem "illicit." A motel room is a blank slate on which you can scribble, sexually speaking, anywhere you want. It is a form of instant amnesia. In its stark, theatrical confines, between its tightly bound sheets, you can start anew every night.

Contrast this to the bed and breakfast we stayed in the following night in Savannah, Georgia. Every room had a name. A last-minute cancellation had made available to us something called the Peach Leather Room. We walked up the wooden steps full of anticipation.

The Peach Leather Room had no peaches, and no leather, but it did have some nice furniture on which lattice doilies had been placed, a spacious bathroom, and a large wooden four-poster bed, which seemed promising. We washed, dressed nicely, and went out to a nice restaurant. After the meal we took a walk under the Spanish moss, got pleasantly lost, and found our way back to the B&B and its creaky staircase leading up to our room.

Like the stairs, the bed creaked. And at some point, as the bed creaked away, I had two disturbing thoughts. One was that surely everyone in this creaky old house could hear this bed creaking. The other was the abstract idea of how many other couples had lain on this bed, making it creak. My thoughts then drifted to Jack Kemp, the college football star turned blow-dried politician. He had been sitting with some other cigar smokers in the lobby. I had watched Jill approach him to offer an excited hello. They had once met some years ago. The politician and his friends were courteous. I wanted their smiling faces and knew a pornographic scroll of images was unfurling behind them.

Bed and breakfasts are on the whole too domestic and calm, and the beds will creak in a scolding, reproachful way, as though you're hurting them. Then you have to face everybody over cornflakes in the morning. In spite of all those romantic frills, they are less romantic, finally, than the sheer free fall of possibility that accompanies an anonymous unprepossessing motel room. Motel: a hotel for motorists, for people on the move, in transition, at large in the world. We wanted to be going places, getting there wasn't the point.

I'VE heard that a true test of a relationship is how you get along on long car trips. "If you can survive this, you can survive anything," said a friend upon hearing of our plans.

With Jill and me the opposite was somehow true. We were good on car trips. In our real lives there were so many variables; we were not married, but we had gone beyond the realm of dating, into the netherworld of "a relationship."

In a relationship you don't question the main fact that you are together. But there are a lot of little questions. The largest one is, will you get married, or will you break up? But then there are these other nettlesome things: At whose place will we spend the night? And, since we don't spend absolutely every night together, which night, in the course of events, will we spend apart? And who is going to say, "I want to spend Tuesday alone?" And who is going to say, "I don't want to be alone on Tuesday! How could you leave me alone on a Tuesday?"

Something about traveling together removes this element. You don't know what will happen next. Once resigned to that fact, the present looms up and grabs you. You have to either love it or hate it.

In a car, the two of you are in it together, there is nowhere else to turn, no friend with whom you can blow off steam over a drink. All the emotions—love, anger, irritation—come quickly to the surface. In such a compressed space there are definitely going to be fights. And we did have fights. What were they about? Their surface substance eludes me now. The actual point of contention between lovers when they fight is always so hard to remember, because it's just a buoy on the surface of the ocean indicating the real subject somewhere deep below. Down there lies the undersea topography that dictates the currents, the storms, the cataclysmic waves. You can't really describe this undersea landscape. Dreams, arguments, expressions of love, speechless attacks of lust, they all provide a kind of silhouette.

On the road, the fights are tropical in their intensity, and also their brevity. We fought, and we had to work through the fights. Being on a road trip is like being stuck together on a moving desert island. Along with the spectacular overheated fights come the spectacularly overheated make-ups. And a car is so useful for this. A car is like a portable bedroom and living room and attic, all in one. You become expert at searching out the tiny unused lanes of the world, all beckoning you for a brief siesta.— The service roads leading to graveyards, the dirt roads leading to meadows on which only a few inquiring cows are around to witness you leaning back in the passenger seat.

And then there were quiet moments when the car hummed smoothly down the road and Jill slept in the passenger seat. In some ways I felt my love for her most intensely when I was driving and she was sleeping, beautifully at rest and safe by my side. I don't know why this moved me. In hindsight, I would say that, however much you are overcome with tenderness at such moments, it's probably a bad sign if your favorite time with your girlfriend occurs when she is sleeping.

JILL'S tirade among the lobster traps eventually ended. I finally got her back in the car and we were quiet for a long time. Then we made a snap decision to detour through the pine forest over to Naples, Florida, and head up the Gulf Coast. In Naples the air was crisper, the houses pink, and old people drove slowly down the streets in brand-new Cadillacs. We drove up the coast and stopped at the Sarasota State Fair and bought several pairs of cheap sunglasses. Then we got down to the serious business of driving home. We drove nonstop.

A hundred miles outside of New York, at three in the morning, a blizzard struck. The snow was momentous, each flake as big as a fist. In the southbound lane, we passed a truck on its side. It was just a glimpse through the snow; something large and immobile. After that, all we had as evidence of what we thought we saw was the long processional of trucks stuck in traffic, inching along in the opposite direction, their outlines lit by lights. They were melancholy, like a herd of elephants that knew one of their own had been wounded.

On our side of the highway, the trucks slowed in the blizzard but did not stop. Neither did we. I couldn't see ten feet out the windshield, but stopping was not an option we discussed for more than a moment. Movement was a drug we weren't ready to forsake. Instead we found a truck and nestled in its slow-moving wake. Its red brake lights were our only compass. It was exhilarating. At that moment, when huge trucks were careening out of control, when the car was fishtailing in the mounting snow, and when visibility was a matter of feet, I felt incredibly *with* Jill in that small, enclosed space. We had found a place of safety, however temporary. On we went. The snow finally abated. By the time we reached the Holland Tunnel, it had turned to rain.

And we awoke late the next morning to find a city bathed in bright sunlight. Other than the occasional moist puddle, there was nothing to indicate that a huge catastrophic blizzard had poured over the interstate in the hours before dawn. It was as though the storm, and maybe the whole trip, had been a dream. Now the storm was over, and in a month or so we would be over, too. Now, when I look back at it, it's the road trips I most remember, when the double life of ambivalence left me. For all those days spent speeding down the road we had been completely and irrefutably together. We'll always have that.

THE
TRYOUT

★

38 years old

I SAT IN THE CAR BEFORE THE TRYOUT. MY SNEAKERS were on the seat next to me. The parking lot was crowded and more cars were pulling in. The tryout was being held on a college campus whose name often appeared in the newspaper. The New York Knicks had their practices here. Here was the place where those gruff transactions between a player and journalist took place, the results of which were sprinkled through the next day's paper like little nuggets of gold.

The college, SUNY Purchase, is not distinguished for its basketball program. It is just a place with a basketball court but it is where the Knicks practice and so everyone pulling up in their cars wasn't arriving at just any basketball facility but at the place where the professional basketball players they read about in newspapers pull up in their cars, music blasting.

The Westchester Wildfire, a newly formed franchise of the United States Basketball League, was holding open tryouts. About eighty people were in the gym warming up, in spite of the $150 fee. The gym was filled with big guys, medium-sized guys, guys with jump shots, guys with muscles, white guys, black guys, pink, yellow, and brown guys, everyone loosening their bodies and playing that little mantra in their heads, a personalized version of, "I know I can I know I can I know I can."

Some of these guys had played for top-flight universities. They had seen the big time. But a fair number were playground all-stars for whom the tryout was a kind of one-day basketball fantasy camp, an opportunity to run up and down in the same gym where the Knicks practice. I kept glancing around to see the star attraction of the day, John Starks, the New York Knick whom the Westchester Wildfire had named as their first head coach. Starks kept a low profile during the morning session, haunting the sidelines briefly and then appearing upstairs in a booth overlooking the gym. At one point another familiar face from years past appeared next to him up there—Jeff Van Gundy, former coach of the Knicks, his eyes less dark than usual, his hair—that incredible catastrophe of implants—subdued on his head.

I glimpsed Starks for just a moment, gray shirt and shorts, his white socks pulled up neatly to cover his ankles, smiling while someone patted him on the shoulder. Then a whistle was blown, the terse shriek that is the basketball equivalent of a judge pounding his gavel, and the tryout began.

★　★　★

THERE is a masochistic thrill in witnessing the undeniable fact of your physical inadequacy. Maybe that was why I was there, to be reminded of my place in the athletic cosmos. But I was also there because, like all the other dreamers who were not Division I players—and that was a lot of us—I was secretly convinced that I could perform a little magic. We all have different tricks but they ended with the same result—the ball goes in the hole.

We began drills. We ran up and down the court passing the ball back and forth. The dreamers had to keep up with players who could run twice as fast, jump twice as high . . . and who themselves could not keep up with the very best players on the floor, who could run twice as fast, jump twice as high . . . and who *themselves* were long shots to make the team, whose best players were long shots to make an NBA team.

Right away we were split into three groups. The serious contenders, immediately recognizable by height, demeanor, and reputation, were in one group. Everyone else composed the other two. We did running drills, passing drills, three-man weaves, fast-break drills. Everyone strained and pushed themselves to their limit. To try as hard as you can is an interesting thing; interesting to do the trying and interesting to see other people try. As hard as I could was too slow, too close to the ground. I watched a guy, not too much taller than six feet, race down the floor and then take off just inside the foul line, sending a crashing dunk through the hoop with two hands. As hard as he could was impressive. Surely this guy will make the team, I thought.

He didn't.

The last thing we did was break into small groups to play three-on-three, and it was here, finally, that I got to do the tricks. Every time I scored or blocked a shot I thought: Did anyone see that? But I knew it was too late. One guy I played against was rail-thin, light-skinned, with a spray of freckles across his face. He wore a white headband and his Afro rose up behind his head like an off-kilter chef's hat. I posted him up and felt his heart beating. His chest literally thumped against my back. I'd never felt that before. Why was his heart beating like that?

Perhaps it was sheer physical effort and adrenaline, but I think it was panic. All of us in our group had failed to distinguish ourselves. We had seen what the competition was like. It was clear we were outclassed. Some illusion had been shattered. It was not a great loss, the sting wasn't too bad, but the moment did require a fleeting acknowledgment that we had allowed ourselves to hope, to dream a little.

Most of the players were cut before lunch, including me. Dream over.

THE remaining players came back for an afternoon session, and I stuck around to watch. There was a good deal of talent on the floor. Zach Marbury, Stephon's younger brother, was there, as was Brian Reese from North Carolina, Kitwana Rhymer from U Mass, and Lenny Cook, the high school player who declared for the recent NBA draft and then failed to get drafted.

Cook was now in the strange limbo of leagues like the USBL, where sub-NBA players operate on a barnstorming circuit, hoping to develop their skills, attract attention, and move up to the NBA.

Hoping, in other words, for the spectacular moth-to-butterfly transformation experienced by John Starks.

After playing at Oklahoma State, Starks played briefly in the CBA, the World Basketball League, and at one point was bagging groceries in Tulsa before making it to the Golden State Warriors and then the Knicks, where, in spite of his Oklahoma accent, he embodied a hyperactive energy and enthusiasm that seemed to speak to the whole city, at least for a little while.

When a TV crew stood in front of Cook during the warmups and posed the question, "Lenny, do you still think you have a shot at the NBA?" his answer was inaudible. But I'd like to think it was: "Most definitely."

This phrase—"most definitely"—was for a period of time the touchstone of everything John Starks said. He used it as the preface to every statement, the beginning of every answer. It was a linguistic crutch and philosophy of life rolled into one. It was the essence of Starks. He had some speech coaching somewhere along the line; at some point someone must have told him to drop the phrase.

When Starks spoke at the midday press conference he was smooth, composed, and articulate. He sat beside the team's owner, Gary Lieberman. Lieberman was a former Bear Stearns banker and now a hedge fund manager. He was a small man with delicate nail-bitten hands. His eyes were rimmed with pink. He was a banker and there was something about him that suggested that this whole enterprise, owning this minor league basketball team, was an attempt to let go of a prudence that was deeply ingrained in his soul. The prudence of a skinny kid who got beat up a lot and went on to make a lot of money as a money guy.

Starks sat there. Prudence is not the word that one associates with John Starks. He was subdued and chose his words carefully. He said how happy he was to be here, where he spent so many years with the Knicks. He was relaxed in blue shorts and a gray Westchester Wildfire polo shirt, and looked remarkably unchanged from his days in New York. His round, almost babyish forehead was as smooth as ever, the pensive eyes familiar, as was the puckish, bashful, mischievous smile. He spoke about how playing for Pat Riley and Jeff Van Gundy had taught him a lot about what it takes to win. When asked about the talent he had seen so far, he said, "It's too early to tell right now. You can get a sense of a player's athletic ability and you can see their offense, but you can't really see how well they're going to play defense until you see them in a full-court game."

Sports journalism is probably the most overfunded activity in the world. So much effort in connection with such meager rewards! These little nuggets one hopes to get from players. It's like asking the magician how he does it.

With Van Gundy in the house one almost expected to see Patrick Ewing stride in. Starks said he hoped his former teammates would put in appearances. "There's a host of players and former coaches who will come by, and I welcome that, because I learn, too."

Asked if he would consider suiting up, he said, "I won't pull a Michael Jordan," and smiled.

Lieberman, the team owner, roamed the sidelines during the afternoon session and explained the secret method he used for acquiring Starks as a coach. "I was watching the Ewing retirement ceremony and I saw John interviewed. He said he wanted to coach, so I called him up."

The afternoon workout was intense. There were running drills and then four-on-four fast-break drills. Jerrold Mcrae of Northwestern and Greg Stevenson of Richmond were standouts, both of them throwing down gigantic dunks in traffic. Craig Austin, from Columbia, and last year's Ivy League Player of the Year, had a calm, distant, almost Zenned-out expression the whole time. He had a wandering eye, which was an odd attribute for a guy whose game revolved around a jump shot.

Zach Marbury looked a lot like his brother Stephon—the round head, the terse, almost militant hand gestures, directing traffic, the faintly fascistic air of a martinet. But he did not have his brother's game. During warm-ups, he wore a sweat suit and sneakers that gleamed with newness. There was a swagger to him. But on the court a certain timidity appeared, as though he were ashamed, slightly, that his talents didn't live up to the older brother who was giving him the money for the new clothes.

Then there was the long-faced, ominous, and extremely skinny seven-foot-two Terry Sellers, in his late twenties, out of Compton, now residing in New Jersey. His thin legs were nicked and scratched. One of the coaches, asked why Sellers didn't have a higher basketball profile, said, "The streets got him," and shook his head sadly. I had a vision of him literally falling into a hole.

In an empty hallway near the lockers I bumped into Lenny Cook, six-foot-five but just eighteen, having an emotional conversation with a small man in a gray suit carrying a briefcase.

"I'll give you two hundred dollars out of every week's paycheck!" said Cook.

"Listen, I can't help you," said the man.

"I'll give you two hundred dollars out of my paycheck every week, I swear!"

Oh, God, I thought, what? Agent? Loan shark? I got a glimpse of the small man's brittle dyed black hair. He had loan shark hair.

"I'll give you three hundred dollars every week! Please!" His voice rang with emotion, the emotion of a kid.

"Hey, listen," said the man, who was very small. "I'm already in two thousand dollars so far for your travel, your hotel, I can't do any more!"

The man could have been an agent or an owner, it was unclear.

I walked away. It was a random snippet that made the distance between the promise of the NBA and the reality of getting there seem very large. Seeing Starks roaming the sidelines of his old practice facility and knowing what he had accomplished—he was an All-Star, he dunked on Jordan!—was a pure example of Most Definitelyness.

In a way, the whole tryout was John Starks Impersonation Day. Everyone wanted to be like John.

ADDICTED

TO

LOVE

★

34 years old

1.

I was driving through the desert on a bright Arizona day on my way to visit the sex addicts. I was going as a journalist, but this is a subject from which it is hard to keep your distance. I was headed toward a private clinic called The Meadows, in Wickenburg, not far from Phoenix, which under the direction of psychologist Patrick Carnes has developed into one of the leading programs in the country for the treatment of sex addicts. Boundaries are important here, I told myself. I was entering the zone of "helping." The whole place would be brimming with help. And there was a temptation, I had to admit, to help myself to some help. Did I need some help?

Boundaries, I said to myself. *Boundaries.*

But there were no boundaries out here. The skies were blue, the desert was vast and dotted with tumbleweed and cactus, and I was speeding down a narrow strip of pavement in a rented car, thinking about sex; not good sex, or bad sex, but *overwhelming* sex. Sex—the drug.

It was Carnes who first coined the phrase "sex addict" back in 1983, and developed a system of treatment modeled after the 12-step program of Alcoholics Anonymous. First, the addict has to admit he or she is powerless over her addiction. And then he or she has to appeal to a "higher power" for help.

So I was thinking, essentially, about sex and God. The vast desert all around me didn't seem large enough to encompass all the possible variations on these two themes. Then, in the middle of nowhere (actually about forty miles south of a town called Nowhere) I saw a sign that brought things into focus and made me laugh.

It read: "Detention Center. Do Not Pick Up Hitchhikers."

I immediately imagined escaped sex addicts standing by the side of the road next to a cactus, trying to wave down the passing cars. I should say very clearly that The Meadows is not a detention center. People are there because their lives have spiraled out of control. They've lost their jobs, their marriages, they've been arrested, or come within a hair's breadth of those things happening. They *want* to be there. There is no chain-link fence. If you want to leave, you can take a cab; you don't have to hitchhike.

But still, I liked imagining them lined by the side of the road, and wondered what they might look like. Maybe they'd look like Kate Moss, whose recent rehabilitation for drink and drugs was rumored to include treatment for sex addiction. Or maybe they'd look like Bill Clinton. You can't think about sex addiction for even a second without speculating about President Clinton, or vice versa. Maybe they'd look like you. Maybe they'd look like me.

I'D BEEN reading the literature of self-destruction through sex. Carnes's books are laced with case histories. His prose is very simple and has an almost incantatory quality. He strings one anecdote into the next and it's like listening to a series of dysfunctional bedtime stories. Jack and Jill went up the hill and had compulsive sex with strangers. It's as though you are hiding behind the curtain in a doctor's office. "Del was a lawyer. Brilliant, charming, and witty. His wife and three children were proud of his accomplishments. However, Del's public visibility was creating a problem because he was also a sexual addict. His double life included prostitution, porno bookstores, and affairs."

Or: "Chris . . . was an addict whose cruising was fused with her professional life as a consultant in urban planning . . . her life was filled with seminars, conferences, and workshops. They served as a cover for her other life."

There is no question that there are men and women (and, according to Carnes, one of three sex addicts is a woman) whose relationship to sex has caused their lives to spiral out of control. But then again, sex addiction? How about chocolate addiction? How about golf addiction? People solemnly filing into MBA (Marx Brothers Anonymous) declaring, "I am powerless to resist my desire to watch Groucho."

I imagined cars anxiously speeding past the escaped sex addicts as they tried to hitch a ride. It made me laugh. Then I looked up in the rearview mirror and caught a glimpse of myself. I stopped laughing.

2.

There are no meadows at The Meadows. The small cluster of bungalows and one-story buildings looks, at first glance, like a community college campus, or maybe a nursing home. There are a few patches of grass and a pine tree in their midst, neat walkways lead from one building to the next, and from almost every vantage point there is a view of the desert; the very sight of it makes you feel meditative and small.

I'm greeted by John, director of marketing at The Meadows. Although I don't put the question to him directly, I can tell that John is not a member of recovery culture. Unlike all the counselors here, he's not a reformed addict; he could well be marketing director for a consortium of podiatrists or a country club. But he has a sympathetic face, a sort of fixed expression of empathy that must be extremely useful in his wanderings among people who crave empathy.

The first thing we do is get some lunch in the sunny cafeteria. The patients sit at tables chatting, a youngish bunch who are suffering from an assortment of ailments like drug addiction and alcohol addiction and sex addiction and eating disorders, with the odd gambling addict thrown in. I cast a longing gaze at them. I'd been told repeatedly that I would not be able to talk with them, and John seems quite jumpy to see me even look in their direction.

After lunch John takes me to meet Bob Fulton and Maureen Canning, the primary sex addict counselors. While John goes in to tell them I'm here, I wander over to a small and somewhat forlorn little gazebo with a sign on it that says, "Smoking Hut."

The Meadows understandably takes a stern view of all stimulants—caffeine can't be found in any form—but their policy is to treat nicotine addiction last. The structure and placement of this hut, however, makes it clear that smoking is not encouraged. A few plain benches are arranged around a tall cement ashtray that juts up in the middle, as though it were some absurd altar of grime at which the smokers are forced to worship.

A guy with a bandanna comes up to me and asks if I'm in the survivors' group. I tell him I'm not, and he walks away. But, in Meadows-speak, I *am* a survivor—because the thing that survivors have survived, it turns out, is their childhood.

THE first thing I notice when I walk into Bob and Maureen's office is something that resembles a large red Wiffle ball bat, though this one is made of foam rubber and canvas and seems designed more for bopping someone on the head (in a cathartic, constructive way) than for hitting a ball.

Bob was a Catholic priest for seventeen years. Maureen has a nice smile, but as we talk I notice that every now and then her blink is a little delayed. It only happens once or twice, as though something she has just said, some small tidbit of information, has triggered a powerful memory and caused her to momentarily freeze, the eyelid paused at half-mast. When I ask what their respective addictions were, Bob says he was an alcoholic, and Maureen says she was a sex addict. Her slow-motion blink seems like the old, reptilian sex addict within struggling to come out.

Bob and Maureen are in charge of the process by which sex addicts look toward their past to discover the origins of their behavior—the central tenet of sex addiction being that sex addicts suffered abuse, in some form, as children.

"We look at the underlying trauma in their lives," says Maureen. "Each patient starts by writing out an autobiography up to age seventeen."

Part of me thinks this is only slightly better than going to a palm reader, and part of me really likes the idea of taking a thirty-minute synopsis of my own life and handing it over to a couple of experts who can discern where, exactly, I got fucked up. This place was to psychoanalysis what Evelyn Wood is to reading.

"When they present their autobiographies," says Maureen, "what I'm listening for are the trauma bonds. What were the messages they got, and how are they playing them out today? And then, throughout treatment, I'm constantly tying their current behaviors back to their original wounding."

"Sometimes this is an explicit wound, such as sexual molestation. Other times it is more covert, but has a similarly corrosive effect, though less like a hurricane than like a wave slowly eroding the rock that it crashes against. An example of this might be the way a father looks at his daughter's breasts, or his repeated requests for a massage. Or a mother who shames her son for having caught him masturbating. Or a mother who *doesn't* shame her son for having caught him masturbating. (Hanging out at the The Meadows, one comes to feel that parenting is a futile enterprise.)

"Once the patient starts to draw correlations between the past and present, they start to heal the trauma," says Maureen. She makes it sound easy. You figure out your trauma, and then it goes away.

But, Maureen adds, "It's not something we're going to be able to heal in thirty-five days. What we *can* do is bring up the consciousness around those issues and then start to give them tools to deal with the addiction as they continue to work on the trauma. Everyone who comes through here has some kind of wounding and trauma, not necessarily sexually, but around their self-esteem issues, and their sense of who they are, and their sense of self-worth."

To think of a sex addict is to conjure an image of an out-of-control man succumbing at every turn to the culture's avalanche of provocative sexual stimuli. For women the best one can do is imagine a *Looking for Mr. Goodbar* scenario. It just sounds like a more male affliction.

The Meadows has a capacity for seventy patients at a time; the norm is around fifty, of which maybe a quarter are there to be treated for sex addiction. At the moment, only one of the sex addict inpatients is a woman.

"Unfortunately, we don't see a lot of women," says Maureen. "Probably only ten percent of the people who come in for sex addiction are women. Which is very disheartening to me, because that means that women are not getting the treatment they need."

So what is the destructive behavior women engage in?

"They have affairs," says Maureen.

And the very definition of an affair is fairly elastic. "We're seeing more and more women going on the Internet, having romantic exchanges, and then meeting people and having, ultimately, sexual affairs.

"Usually," she says, "what brings a woman here are the consequences of their behavior: facing a divorce; losing their job; health risks; depression; suicidal thoughts; unable to get up out of bed; unable to function, to take care of the children."

Whether male or female, sex addicts make sex, and their own sexuality, the main feature of their self-image. "At the very core of a sex addict's being, they feel worthless," says Bob. "The sense of who they are is not fully developed, because the parents haven't been there to give it to them. The abandonment fuels shame, and shame fuels addiction. And so what will undo it is the trauma resolution around the abandonment wounds."

I'm really starting to despair. On one hand, I find this interesting: People who were in some way traumatized by their formative experiences with their parents (a group that includes, I think it is fair to say, *everybody*, but I'll leave that alone for now) need to constantly reaffirm their worth by having sex with other people. And this compulsive sex makes them feel better, and then awful, and they have to do it all over again.

On the other hand, what Bob and Maureen are saying seems to be a new age version of Philip Larkin's famous line, "They fuck you up. Your mum and dad, they may not mean to but they do." And he didn't get $35,000 for that poem. So, in this uncharitable mood, I ask about the red rubber bat.

"It's called a Bataka," says Maureen. "We use it for anger

work. A lot of times a patient has a lot of anger that they have never been able to express to the perpetrator. We have them sit across from an empty chair, raise the bat, and say, 'I'm really *angry* with you,' and then beat the empty chair. So that they're able to let that emotion out in a safe way.

"And then once they're moving the anger out, the sadness and the pain will start to come up, and then the tears. And when that happens, you're really getting down into the pain of that little kid.

"When a child's been traumatized he literally freezes, because he can't assimilate what has happened. And we try and get those feelings out. I call it 'unthawing.' And so when they open that door, a stream of emotions come pouring out, and healing can begin."

So for the sex addict, shame is both wound and medicine. The addiction is circular: Sex takes you out of your feelings, but it works like a drug, and when the effect has worn off, the only thing that can placate the ensuing shame and guilt is more sex. "It's almost like the addict is a separate part of yourself," says Bob.

This is the central metaphor of sex addiction: Dr. Jekyll and Mr. Hyde. The shame the addicts feel about their secret life, the lengths they will go to in order to keep it a secret, and also the strange, almost pathological desire they have to get caught.

AT the end of our meeting I pose the rather personal question that has been nagging at me throughout. It's the sort of question that is bound to creep into your thoughts if you're single and writing about sex addiction, namely: How much sex are you allowed to have had before you have to start worrying about yourself?

"Say you walk into an ice-cream store and there are a hundred flavors," I say. "Is it all right to taste a few different ones?"

"Just because there are a hundred flavors doesn't mean you have to taste them all," says Bob. "If you do, what you've precluded is the healthy intimacy and self-realization that you get when you're not fucking the whole world. You can look at the one flavor that you have and get to know it in relationship to you."

"One?" I said, somewhat grievously, suddenly feeling very literal-minded. "You mean a healthy person will go through life having tasted chocolate, but never vanilla?"

"I wouldn't press it into an absolute," says Bob.

"How about chocolate, vanilla, cherry, pistachio, butter pecan, and Concord grape?"

Maureen and Bob are now looking at me with a detached and somewhat professional expression on their faces. It strikes me that this is the expression they must use when a patient begins some sort of cathartic breakdown, a litany of confessions and laments. I pull myself together.

"So what is a healthy number of flavors?" I ask. "Five?"

"What's healthy is being in touch with one's own development; knowing what is motivating one's own behavior. For me it might be three flavors. For someone else, it may be they have twelve; for someone else, it may be the first flavor."

"What about, oh, say, twenty-five?"

"For somebody it might be twenty-five. And if it's twenty-five, I would tend to think that there were things blocking, that many of those encounters were not a total engagement, that many of them were a way of self-medicating."

I nod in agreement with this subtle reproach and then I remember, from out of the blue, reading about a piece of advice that the magician Rickey Jay once received from his mentor. "I really want to know how to improve my technique and performance," the magician had said, referring to his magic tricks. To this the mentor had responded, "Fuck many woman."

This exchange popped into my head, a kind of retort, but I did not share it with Bob and Maureen, who I didn't think would appreciate its grumpy, horny wisdom. And anyway, I thought, what is a magician but a kind of escape artist? Someone who makes things dissappear?

3.

The one case study that I found truly persuasive did not appear in any of Carnes's books; it was a memoir by the poet and English professor Michael Ryan called *Secret Life.* The only photograph of the author appears on the back cover: a happy five-year-old boy sitting on the lawn. The picture was taken by a neighbor, a young man name Bob Stoller, who was also a pederast, and who, using his photography as cover, abused Ryan regularly for a year, starting with the day the picture was taken. Ryan's prose is cool and unsentimental, and the bulk of his book is devoted to his youth and young adulthood, the bumbling but not hugely remarkable path of a smart, rebellious Catholic boy with a loving mother and an alcoholic father. Apart from the description of his molestation, it is a book that one might call charming, and yet in its details one can see an insidious pattern of deviant, unhealthy sexuality develop, like a photograph slowly materializing in a darkroom.

Describing his groping encounters with an early girlfriend who wouldn't sleep with him, he writes, "I did not find this [rolling around] erotic, but sex was only erotic when it was bad, and this was love, and love was good."

This relatively innocent revelation comes toward the end of the book, and for a moment I thought: Well, so what? Good sex has always been, somehow, bad.

But it's a short narrative leap from that relatively innocent observation to this: "I was certainly a magnet for some women, as some women were for me—suicidal women for whom sex was both validation and self-annihilation, an intense temporary escape from being themselves. . . . Their hunger is what made them sexy to me and, no doubt, vice versa. We always at least half hated each other, the half that was a mirror."

And not long after that, he is engaging in absurdly compulsive sex, his marriage falls apart, he is fired from his professorial job at Princeton, and only when he finds himself in the midst of a road trip to see a friend's fifteen-year-old daughter, whom he is intent on seducing, does he pull off to the side of the road and have the epiphany that eventually leads him into the sort of 12-step recovery program that Carnes advocates.

Reading Ryan's evocative book convinced me that Carnes is on to something in identifying certain patterns of sexual behavior, where they come from, and what might be done to stop them.

But then again, where do you draw the line? Reading

Carnes's work, you can't help but constantly look out for echoes of your own experience. And it's likely you'll find them.

"The addict," writes Carnes, "can transform even the most refined forms of nudity into his own particular fusion of loneliness and arousal."

That's a nice phrase. As it happens, I'm prepared to admit that I can take many things—refined or nude or neither—and transform it into my own particular fusion of loneliness and arousal. But I don't know if that's such a bad thing. Sex is, by its very nature, a kind of counterattack on loneliness. The two are somehow entwined.

Finally, there is the fundamental metaphor that Carnes has established for the sex addict, which provides Ryan with his title: *Secret Life*. Each sex addict contains a good self and a bad, secret self. The addicts don't so much engage in sex as *enter* it, as they would a secret chamber; they walk around in a kind of sleepwalking trance.

But isn't this also an accurate description of sex itself? Its transformative power? People lose themselves. They fall out of their own persona and enter into this other self, more wild and voracious or tender or delicate or angry or mirthful than their normal, real, walking-around-the-office, "Good morning!" self. That wild transformation is half the delight of sex, isn't it?

4.

God, or its approximation, is a weird presence in 12-step culture and, therefore, The Meadows. In order to begin recovery you have to accept the presence of a "higher power."

Joe Pack Arnold is The Meadows' spiritual counselor, and his office is evidence of how a "higher power" could mean just about anything. The walls are festooned with a variety of religious objects: A cross hangs from a leather necklace, a brass menorah gleams in the afternoon light, a Buddha meditates in the corner, and there are quite a few Native American objects with feathers attached. His office is feathery.

"I try to get the patients in touch with their spirit, to help 'em to experience intimacy as a spiritual experience," he says in his soothing drawl.

Arnold has about him the strange transcendent vibe of someone whose concerns are metaphysical more than physical. Frizzy gray hair sprouts out from beneath his fishing hat. He has sleepy, melancholy eyes—you could call them bedroom eyes, but given the circumstances that might not be appropriate—that are enlarged by a pair of enormous glasses, and a face that reminds me (in a nice way) of a Cabbage Patch doll. He speaks with a languorous Louisiana accent.

"If they're open to it, we talk a lot about a Higher Power outside the self; a source of energy beyond what we know in our mechanized society; God, if you will."

And what if you won't?

"They're usually the patients I enjoy the most, because they don't bring a lot of baggage with 'em. We do little simple things. Like I have 'em stand on the road down here and make eye contact with a mountain peak five minutes a day. They just look out there. They make contact with something outside of themselves. Or we take a walk. Not a power walk, like Hillary [Clinton] does, but just a walk. You know, just walk around— and listen, look, and see and smell, and see what happens to you. The desert is alive with a lot of things and they become aware of that. One of the things that I push," he continues, "is that whatever you believed was working for you in the past, if you'll do the opposite, something might happen that's better. So if somebody comes in here walking around with a Bible open all the time, I might suggest they read something else."

What might you suggest?

"Well, I might suggest that they read a novel."

Like what?

"Oh, John Updike," he says.

The king of infidelity! Maybe they have a full shelf of Philip Roth in the library as well! He must see this in my face, because he adds, "Or maybe Faulkner." It strikes me that all three of these writers, should you subject them to a Carnes-style evaluation, would be ideal candidates for The Meadows.

I conclude by asking about President Clinton, whose aura is so strongly felt at The Meadows I feel they ought to have an oil portrait of the man over the front door with a little sign saying, "This Could Be You."

"Clinton is a textbook addict," says Arnold. "He grew up in a broken home; his father was an alcoholic; his mother practically raised him; he came from nothing; he's brilliant, which didn't work in his favor, 'cause even though his sex addiction has been so obvious over the years, he's been able to rise above everything, and there's been no intervention. I don't think he'll act out again while he's President . . . but I think he'll act out again.

"If nothing else, he's raised an awareness throughout the country," Arnold continues. "There are a lot of spouses out there watching TV and thinking: Oh, my gosh—Charlie's exactly like the President! We gotta do something about Charlie!"

5.

At last I meet Patrick Carnes, the father, as it were, of sex addiction. He is a fine-looking man, with broad shoulders, a ruddy complexion, and a widow's peak that gives him a slightly roosterish aspect—he has the radiant good health of the early riser. His eyes are bright blue and slightly crossed. He gazes at me with a mixture of forbearance and suspicion. Journalists are not his favorite species.

For a long time he and his specialty have suffered under the slings and arrows of giggles. His books are littered with moments of frustration and exasperation with the media and the culture as a whole; sex addiction is his baby, and every snigger and joke at its expense must have felt like a personal attack.

So these post-Lewinsky days are a time of heady vindication for Patrick Carnes. The whole country has spent a solid year fixated on someone who is clearly not in control of his own sexual urges.

"Bill Clinton has helped a lot of people," he begins cautiously, and then adds, "inadvertently. Before the Monica Lewinsky stuff blew up, we probably were thirty years behind alcoholism in terms of public understanding. Now we're only fifteen years behind."

So is Clinton a sex addict?

"I don't know. One of the things a professional looks for is: Does this person know that something is going to cause them a great deal of pain and loss that they cannot afford—and they consistently proceed to do that, anyway? That would be a sign of addiction."

Throughout my readings of Carnes's books I was always on the lookout for signs that he was, at heart, a kind of sex-negative scold; that the concept of sex addiction was really a way of taking the whole sexual revolution and turning it into a mental illness; that it was a cover for Puritanism. But whenever it seems like that might be the case, he confounds that notion by advocating *more* sex, not less.

"It is clear that sexual health should not be exploitative or judgmental or negative," he wrote. "Rather, the foundation for healthy sexuality starts with acceptance, abundance, and exploration."

So how is one to decipher where a healthy, *abundant* sexuality ends and where an unhealthy, desperate, medicating sexuality begins?

"The question is whether the obsession is interfering with your life," says Carnes.

To this I imagine a chorus of guys saying, "It's not interfering with my life, it *is* my life!" But this doesn't seem like a productive image to share with Carnes.

"What about affairs?" I ask instead. "An affair will definitely interfere with your life. If there is an affair in a marriage, does that mean the partner who had an affair is a sex addict?"

"I would guess that forty to fifty percent of relationships in this country end up with an affair somewhere," he says. "Asking how many affairs it takes to make a sex addict is like asking how many drinks does it take to make an alcoholic. It's about a pattern of behavior over the long term, and about how you are living your life.

"Most people realize that they have a problem because there are things that they're doing that they know they can't afford to do . . . and that they persist in doing, anyway. Then they start making promises to themselves to stop, and find that they can't. That's when people know they've crossed the line—when they can't stop having sex."

SEX is an instinct, an appetite as fundamental to our existence as our appetite for food. So can something that is necessary to the survival of our species be an addiction?

Dr. Chester Schmidt is a psychiatrist at the Johns Hopkins sexual behavior consultation unit, and was part of a special task force that deliberated whether to list sex addiction in the DSM. They decided against it.

"In terms of pop psychology, the term 'sex addiction' is very appealing. It just intuitively makes sense to a lay person that certain individuals have an appetite for sex that is greater than the norm. How better to explain that in today's psychological terms than to call it an addiction?

"Carnes's method," he continues, "is to treat sex addiction the same way you would treat substance addiction. Removal from stimulation, detox, twelve-step program, psychological support.

"In medicine the term 'addiction' has a specific pharmaco-logical meaning: Substances taken into the body are active in the brain in such a manner that their removal causes a cascad-ing effect of physiological symptoms known as withdrawal.

"We do not accept the concept that excessive sexual activity is in fact addictive, in the way we use that term."

The great mantra of the recovery movement is that whatever works is good. I ask Schmidt if he is being too pedantic, not seeing the forest for the trees.

"It's hard to say if Carnes's treatments are helpful, because he has never subjected his findings to a peer review journal. He's never done controlled studies. To determine if a treatment or a drug is worth anything, you have to do a controlled study."

But Carnes points out that there are difficult ethical considerations when it comes to applying scientific methods to the real world. "Doing a controlled experiment would mean taking certain people whose behavior puts them in a life-and-death situation, giving them virtually no treatment at all to do a controlled study," he says. "It's a problem of doing scientific research in the real world. What we do instead is follow the behaviors of people who recover and the behavior of people who relapse into the old behavior. It's a different way of profiling what works."

But Schmidt is not fully convinced. "Sex addiction is a facile explanation for an extraordinarily complex set of behaviors," he says. "If you can explain away certain disturbing behaviors with a single diagnosis, it literally catches your breath. You can say: 'I know my problem. I'm a sexual addict!'"

A DESERT sunset is a sight that will have you believing in a higher power almost instantly, and it is against this backdrop that Carnes and I shake hands and say good-bye. Carnes is smiling at me with that expertly beneficent smile, the smile of a minister or a doctor or a hustler. He is not a hustler, but there is something in the "If you're hurting, come to us" embrace of The Meadows that I distrust.

In a way my problem is similar to Schmidt's. It's a question of language, but it's a different objection to Schmidt's clinical specificity: I just can't abide by this exhausting phenomenon by which the recovery movement colonizes every aspect of human experience and makes it something that needs to be cured.

Of all our appetites, sex is the most anarchic. It's where we feel our keenest sense of sin. It rides roughshod over our ethics and our desire to be just to other people. All over the world people build relationships on which so much rests, and the single biggest fault line that can destroy nearly all that hard-won trust is the issue of sexual wantonness, of infidelity; the idea that one of the partners will look outside the relationship to satiate a sexual appetite he or she cannot control.

Carnes's work is interesting for the way it looks at the ways we misuse our sexuality—the way we can use sex as a means of communication, a way of defining ourselves, or simply as a narcotic to numb the discomfort of intimacy—sex that isn't a conduit to intimacy, but a *substitute for* intimacy. The term "sex addiction," however, takes lust and makes it something that needs fixing. It makes pathological that which is part of life. It makes, I suggest, desire a disease.

"Sex addicts are not getting the sexual rewards they want, they're not happy with what they are doing," says Carnes. "If the only way for a woman to be orgasmic is for a man to hurt her, that is not a functional template. We want to help these people have more rewarding sex, it's like helping them rewire themselves."

Carnes, standing against the distant mountains, has a kind of John Wayne, evangelical, last-good-man vibe. His voice is so soothing. He just wants to help. He stands like a sexual Statue of Liberty amid an ocean of sand: Give me your abused, your hurting, your sexually self-destructive. We will rewire you. You wont have to hurt yourself anymore.

There is so much tumult, dissonance, fear, and despair out in the wide world of sex; here the waters are calm. There is no doubt that there are people out there being terribly self-destructive with sex; here they can be "rewired." And in truth, I'm lulled by his vision, comforted somehow. There is just one little qualm. "Couldn't you just change the name?" I want to say. "How about sex compulsion? Sex obsession? Sex depend-ency?" But then, sex addiction by any other name just wouldn't be as sexy.

THE LAST
DAYS OF
SHAKESPEARE
& COMPANY

★

30 years old

BOOKS WERE STACKED IN PILES AROUND MY NEW apartment, looming like weird stalagmites in a cave. They were encroaching from all directions. A bookcase was badly needed, and yet months slid by without a purchase. The absurd stacking of books gave my living space the air of something temporary, an encampment from which one might easily flee. The stacks also suggested a maniacally literate person in the process of becoming more literate, when in fact I rarely opened the books, preferring to stare with morbid fascination at their sheer accumulation.

Then one day, after lunch with my mother at Edgar's on Eighty-fourth Street, I passed Shakespeare & Company booksellers on Broadway, which was busily going out of business in the shadow of Barnes & Noble up the block. I grew up in this neighborhood, and though I no longer live there I still take a proprietary interest in it. Shakespeare & Company was my neighborhood bookstore, where I had my first marathon browsing sessions—those long, stupefied, and slightly depressing perusals. It was where my first book had held a spot on their bestseller list for the better part of a summer (one week at No. 11), the only bestseller list on which it made a dent.

Now signs in the window announced that it was going out of business, steep discounts, etc., and the store, which had come to seem a bit forlorn, was bustling with people. Then I spotted a sign, hastily scrawled and tacked up in the corner. It read: "Bookshelves for Sale."

Never mind that the price was a steep $300 per bookshelf, my heart leapt. In the week that followed I had several phone conversations with Bill Kurland, who owned the store with his brother Steve. Yes, I could buy a bookshelf, but I would have to wait until it was empty of books. They would sell as many as they could, and then close the store to pack up what remained. I would be able to pick up the shelf in the narrow corridor of time between when everything was packed and when they had to turn over the key to the landlord.

For some reason this detail gave me pleasure. New York is a town of commerce, of buying and selling and moving in and being forced out, and in buying my bookshelf I was intersecting with this vicious tide, however peripherally. This was the real world, where the big fish swallow the little fish, and the little fish sells its bookcases to the unquestioning minnow for $300 a shot. I went by the store again, tape measure in hand,

and measured the dimensions of my future possession. The store was still crowded, but now its frayed going-out-of-business edges were showing. It was a depressing scene, but I was determined to be practical and even lighthearted about it. New York is a fast town, and one of the experiences it accelerates is that of nostalgia. Anyone who has grown up in this city, or spent some part of their lives here, has probably seen their neighborhood undergo change both subtle and drastic, and feel tempted to comment on it like an old fogy. For a while every visit to my old neighborhood was punctuated with curmudgeonly remarks about how things have changed, mostly for the worse. I was becoming a Young Fogy. I decided this was unhealthy. I vowed to be upbeat, or at least apathetic, when some gargantuan operation opened up and the city I used to know receded a bit further from view.

The following Saturday I got the call. The store was closed, they were moving out. I found the place in a partly disassembled condition, boxes everywhere—a radio was on loud, broadcasting a Yankees game, and the calm, relaxed voices of the baseball announcers echoing through the place gave it a ghostly, haunted quality. All the wall space, floor to ceiling, was covered with now-empty shelves—dark, forbidding, and, in their massive, all-connected unity, rather beautiful, like rows of cathedral pews set on their sides.

The shelves I wanted, it turned out, were not merely held together by some screws, but were part of one huge intricate and interconnected design. How to dismantle? I took a few stabs at it with my screwdriver, but it was like trying to dig up Sixth Avenue with a Swiss army knife. So I went out to get a small crowbar.

It was a crisp autumn day, and the street was magnificently alive. Broadway, between about Eighty-fourth Street and Seventy-ninth Street, dips a little, like at the bottom of a shallow bowl, and the result is that at any given point you can see the whole throng of people strolling along. I was swept up to Riverside Housewares on Eighty-fourth Street, one of the few stores left in the neighborhood that I can remember from my childhood. It is a fabulously eccentric place, run by Mr. and Mrs. Stern, a Hungarian couple who have surrounded the store's more practical offerings with items culled from antique shops and yard sales far and wide. Even more eccentrically, they *fix* things—lamps, toasters—and are therefore patronized by that vanishing breed of people who believe that if something is broke, you don't throw it out and buy another one, you fix it. My mother belongs to this group.

I went in, got my crowbar, and raced back down to my shelves, which I attacked with savage vigor. Kurland joined me. We yanked and pulled and there was the sound of splintered wood and the creaking, deathly sound of nails being pulled from the place where they had long dwelled. An hour into it, Kurland advised me to give up. Every time we thought we had it figured out, we discovered yet another way that everything was impossibly attached to itself. The shelves, it turns out, had been installed by Kurland's father fifteen years earlier. He was a construction worker, not a cabinetmaker, and he had built these shelves as though he were building a house. He had built them to last.

I refused to give up, possessed as I was with an Ahab-like singularity of mission: Get Shelves. A couple hours of insane yanking and tugging went by. Then the front gate was lifted to allow for some boxes to be moved into a truck, and suddenly the crowd streaming down Broadway had a full view of Shakespeare & Company in its last desiccated form.

And I had a view of them. Some people were utterly indifferent. Others were vaguely curious. And others stopped dead in their tracks, shocked and obviously grief-stricken, as though they had stumbled upon the corpse of a dear friend.

Then there were the crazies: A man rushed into the store and started ranting, "Kmart is moving into Manhattan! It's all going to hell! Kmart!"

An Armand Hammerish type with silver hair, a sharply pressed suit, and a cane walked in and tried to enter into negotiations for the remaining contents of the store. His nurse, in a crisp white uniform, watched patiently for a minute and then dragged him away.

A disheveled woman with rabid eyes and ink-stained hands came in clutching about twenty newspapers to her chest. "If you drive twenty minutes out of Manhattan, in any direction, they think you're crazy! They look at you like you're nuts. And now those people are taking over our last bastion!"

It's just a damn store, I thought. It's hard enough to manage one's own personal life, stay solvent, and have a little left over for a few random acts of generosity—if you take every real estate transaction on Broadway personally, you go nuts. And yet there I stood, encrusted in sweat and dust, working late into the night until those shelves finally came loose. Kurland gave them to me for free, saying I'd earned it. It was a bookshelf, and also a giant wooden memento to my irrational grief at the store's closing. I'd grabbed a bit of Broadway and stuck it in my apartment.

SCENES
FROM A
PLAYGROUND

★

37 years old

1.

One day last fall, when the weather had cooled and summer seemed to be over, I went down to my local basketball court, on Hudson Street between Horatio and Gansevoort Streets, where I've been going for nearly seven years. The court, which is wedged between the West Village, where I live, and the meatpacking district, is on the loose circuit of courts upon which Players, as it were, like to play. But it looked a little emptier than usual. The players there were mostly those diehards whose compulsion to play basketball is somehow suspicious, betraying logic.

"Basketball junkie." That's a phrase you don't

hear much anymore. It's a bit morbid, but there is some truth to the formulation.

I played a few games and then, after nearly everyone had gone home, I lingered to shoot around in the strangely early dusk.

The trance of the basketball court, into which I had fallen so happily all summer long, was broken. I saw from the inside how the place must look from the outside, beyond the chain-link fence that surrounds it: a wide swatch of asphalt in the middle of the city, with dented-up hoops stuck on it, a playground at one end, a softball diamond at the other, the whole thing populated by dog-walkers, bench-sitters, a few kids and their parents, some derelict types, and some guys in baggy shorts playing basketball, all in a space officially known as John Seravalli Park.

Just then the person I have come to call Crazy Lady approached me, with an unusual expression on her face. "Will you take one of these?" she said, handing me a flier. "It's really important."

The Crazy Lady, whose name, I later learned, is Lana, was not, in fact, crazy. She was just very brave, but the two qualities sometimes blur. I started thinking of her as the Crazy Lady when I arrived at the court one afternoon and found her at the center of a mob of basketball players, defending her kids and their friends against what are normally understood to be the laws of playground.

The issue, as is so often the case, was real estate. There is often a point in the afternoon when a critical mass of players have arrived, and the half-court games move over to the full court. Lana's kids were shooting around on the full-court basket when they were suddenly overrun by the players, the home-boys, all of them itchy to get their hands on the ball.

This is a basic playground scene, the big kids (in this case grown men, mostly) evicting the smaller kids.

Lana has frizzy gray hair, wears sandals and jeans, and smokes cigarettes. Her face often registers a "What in God's name is next?" expression that I associate with city parents. The day of the turf war I arrived to find her standing in the middle of the full court, a cigarette in one hand, a cell phone in the other, and, like Gandhi, refusing to move. She negotiated. Words were exchanged. Voices were raised. Finally, a half-court basket was secured for the kids and, like refugees given a new homeland, they were ushered to their basket before Lana yielded the full court to the mob.

This scene repeated itself several times over the course of the summer, which was how I came to think of her as the Crazy Lady.

This autumn day, however, she approached me with a stack of fliers in her arm and an odd look on her face, as though she had seen a monster. A parking lot across Ninth Avenue from our court had been razed to make way for a new hotel, the sort of place whose ambience and room rate are in keeping with the boutique vibe of the neighborhood, but not in keeping with the giant stretch of gray asphalt on which we stood. The razed parking lot was the footprint of the monster. The monster itself? Well, it was capital. Why use any other word? Something bigger and stronger than us was going to take our park away. According to the flier, the Parks Department was considering a proposal to tear up the playground, resurface it with artificial turf and turn it into a private softball field. The nearby Xavier High School would help pay for the renovation. The gates would be padlocked, the ground green, and there would be soccer practice by day and Little League games by night. Who could argue with that?

Quite a few people, apparently. But the tenor of the flier, and the fact that a community board meeting had been arranged to discuss the proposal, suggested that, unknown to us, wheels had been turning for some time. All summer we had been involved in the drama of our playground while, just like a horror movie, the monster was almost upon us.

2.

Now it's spring. On the first sunny and warm day of the season I went down to the court. There was a game in progress at each of the three half-courts, and a crowd of people waiting to play.

Arriving at a basketball court is a seemingly casual thing, but who actually gets to play is determined by a number of Byzantine rituals involving such things as how well known you are to the regulars, how well respected your game is, how you look, what color you are (and there are a very wide range of colors), how you dress, walk, talk.

But these rules are not written down. They are implicit. They incorporate the rules that pertain to the world outside the playground—the rules enforced by the police, for example—but there are variations, additions, and deletions, and no one on hand with a clipboard and a whistle to enforce them.

This is not gym. One of the more important rules is that, in certain circumstances, there are no rules.

★ ★ ★

THAT first day, everyone was in an unusually friendly mood. I slapped people five. Vague communications were made, along the lines of, "How you been?"

The answers were various words and noises that equated with, "Good."

I saw a guy I recognized go by on a bike, a fiercely quick, whippet-thin kid the color of Turkish coffee, who I have privately nicknamed the Assassin, in part because he is so lethal on offense, and in part because most of the time he wears the expression of someone who is prepared to kill you. Most basketball players exist in a state of mild irritation, like magicians who cannot get a certain trick to go just right. Street ball elevates this irritation to a style, and a lot of people on the court sport a homeboy version of the Travis Bickle line, "You talkin' to me?" as though they were just waiting for someone to piss them off.

"You been playin' ball this winter?" someone asked the guy as he rode by on his bike.

"Yeah," he replied. "In a half-assed way."

The reply was so conversational, almost *affable*, that I had a hard time equating it with the vicious, nasty, elevate-in-your-face style he had on the court, where he often wore a white doo-rag that made him look like a member of the hip-hop division of the Foreign Legion (hence, the Assassin). But just then, on his bike, he seemed like a sweet guy only a few years past teenagerdom.

Glancing around the playground just then, I knew a lot of the guys there. I know how they celebrate when they make a big shot. I know how they run when they are tired. I know what part of the court they like to shoot from. I know if they are good in the clutch or if they choke. I know how they smile when they mean it, and how they smile when they are faking it—that defensive smile you see players make sometimes when something bad has happened and they are smiling to show they don't give a fuck—and how they look when they are trying desperately not to smile because they just made a great move but don't want to make it look like a big deal when, after all, they could do it again in their sleep. I know what their bodies are like, what their strength is, what it takes to stop them, and what they'll do to stop me.

What I don't know are their names, other than a nickname or a first name: Em, Al, Danny, Los. I don't know how old they are or how they make a living. There is actually something nice about this kind of relationship. Everything is stripped down to bare essentials. All you bring is yourself and your game.

I CAME to appreciate the strangeness of this dynamic a long time ago, in the events surrounding a guy named Rich. He was a longtime regular at the basketball court I grew up playing on, up in Riverside Park and Seventy-seventh Street. Rich used to arrive at the court in a shroud of silence, carrying a big shoulder bag. He was very fat. Upon arriving, he would stake out a considerable amount of asphalt (a shade of gray as distinctively New York as a yellow taxi) and proceed to elaborately change into a pair of immaculately clean white tube socks. Then came his game sneakers.

Once he got changed, though, Rich was unsilenceable. He

always called his own "Next" (i.e., he made sure he was a captain so he could pick his own team). He did this as judiciously as any NBA general manager. The thing about these street games is that if you win, you play again. If you lose, you watch. Considering the time and effort of getting to the playground in the first place, there was a lot at stake in winning. Rich wanted to win. Therefore he always refused to put me on his team.

Rich was a trash-talker. He wore a plastic mouth guard, like a football player, but spent half the game with it in his hand or sticking halfway out of his mouth as he did his running commentary. The commentary was usually about the ineffectiveness of the man guarding him. He had quick feet and an exasperatingly soft touch. He would use his bulk to bounce you out of the way and get room for his shot. After it went in, he would remove his mouthpiece and tell you how useless you were.

It takes no effort for me to recall how Rich's body felt when I banged into him in a game. The sound of his voice, the way he ran, the speed with which he shifted from being caustic to being—if the word can be applied to basketball—sweet. He's a perfect example of how, on the basketball court, you can know someone intimately and not know him at all.

One day I went to the court and Rich wasn't there. I didn't even notice his absence until I heard some other guys talking about him.

"When they showed his picture on the late news I didn't recognize him because he looked so much thinner," one of them said. "But then I switched to Channel Eleven and saw their picture and said, 'Oh, shit, it's Rich.' "

It took me a few seconds to realize I had seen Rich that day, too. I'd stopped in front of a newsstand to stare at the picture of a dead body, lying facedown on a subway platform in a pool of blood. It was on the cover of both the *Daily News* and the *New York Post*. In spite of the smudgy black-and-white image, there had been something disturbingly intimate about the picture. Now I knew why.

That evening I got a copy of the *News* and read the whole story. Rich, it turns out, was a token booth clerk at the 145th Street Station. He earned thirty thousand dollars a year. He worked a shift from six A.M. to two P.M. This seemed particularly relevant, since it meant that for all those years I had seen him shortly after he got off work. Rich was single. He was an only child. The paper also ran a picture of his mother. There was no doubt from her expression that her picture had been taken after she learned of his death.

I considered sending Rich's mother a note. But I didn't know what to say to her about her son. That his jump shot was solid from fifteen feet? That he had a soft touch and good hands? I didn't write her, and my description of Rich here is the closest I've ever come to sending the note.*

---

*After this piece was published, I got a letter from a man named Carmelo (ta to) Rodriguez: "I knew Rich. He lived off White Plains Road in the Bronx. Nearby, on Bolton Avenue between Story and Lafayette Avenues, there is a schoolyard where from the early 1970's on, a group of us guys, mostly Puerto Rican, played basketball every Saturday. We were in our mid- or late 20's, married or divorced, many of us with children. Most of us no longer lived in the Bronx but came from Manhattan, Queens, Rockland County, Orange County and New Jersey.

"We were joined by neighborhood guys like Rich, who was then about 16. A soft touch on his short jumper made him deadly. He was already a monster player, a bruiser, but he was also a gentle kid who was sort of adopted on the court. Rich was liked by everyone. Yes, he talked trash because he learned on that schoolyard where affection and love for guys one grew up with was expressed by 'sounding' during a game. Today, the corner of

Meanwhile, nothing changed at the court. The culture of street ball in New York is like the city's population: Some people are fixtures as permanent as a tree. Other people show up out of the blue and then, after a week or a month or a couple of years, disappear without explanation, though usually for reasons less tragic than those that explain the disappearance of Rich.

3.

My game got under way.

I had on my team Monsieur M, a skinny man who had arrived not long ago from Haiti and speaks hip-hop with a French accent. He can jump to the moon, but he has not yet learned not to smile. He doesn't use his smile as a weapon of contempt. When he gets happy, he smiles broadly.

Then there was the Laughing Man. Only a month or so earlier, during a spate of warm weather in March, he suffered a dislocated thumb. "I broke my thumb! I broke my thumb!" he called out, and, in a continuation of the play, he ran right out of the playground in the direction of St. Vincent's Hospital. After he was gone, I saw that blood had splattered on the gray asphalt, a spray of red drops slowly turning to brown. That was an unusual injury, but it highlighted the fact that people get hurt out here.

A month later he was back, with white tape around his injured finger, in his irrepressibly good mood.

Bolton and Lafayette Avenues is named Richard A. Daily Square in honor of his memory. His mother hangs out with the guys in the schoolyard every Saturday, sitting on a beach chair, smoking a cigarette. In June, there is a barbeque in Rich's honor."

The Laughing Man has one of those iron-hard upper bodies (he usually plays without a shirt), and he can jump quickly; he's like a socially well-adjusted Dennis Rodman, with a touch of Karl Malone. The Laughing Man is also a father. A little girl who was standing near him one day as he changed into his sneakers and socks announced loudly, "Daddy, those socks stinky!"

Between Monsieur M and the Laughing Man, it might seem like everyone down at the court is exceptionally friendly and in a good mood, but that is not the case.

Our third member is a young man named D. He has the baggiest shorts on the court and, when he can bring himself to shoot it, a nice jump shot. In between games, you get a glimpse of the fantasy highlight reel that D is always starring in as he practices dunks. In game situations, however, with people barking at him, people watching, with the pressure on, D tends to, shall we say, withdraw. The situation reminds me of a Gatorade commercial whose tag is, "It's what you have in you." But that is not true, or only partially true. It's how much of what is in you that you can get *out* of you. That's true of both sports and writing. He's probably the only guy about whom one could say, "He doesn't shoot enough."

The fourth member of my team is me: At six feet five and a half, a high school and Division III college career behind me, I am, in my own way, a basketball poster boy. In every basketball poster there are two essential components: The first is someone flying high through the air in the middle of some amazing, gravity-defying move, usually a dunk. The second is the person, often partially obscured, being dunked on. I fulfill the latter role.

We won our first game. Monsieur M was the star of the show, skying for rebounds and hitting his jump shot. The team we beat was comprised of guys about whom I could give thumbnail sketches, quick scouting reports, some essential details about personality, and whose name I hardly knew.

The next team was a tough, athletic squad comprised of longtime locals, among them the Litigator. His real name was Dennis but he was the Litigator to me because he was always manipulating the score, arguing calls, pressing for any advantage. Once, when I referred to him as the Litigator out loud, some guy next to me on the sidelines said, "What are you talking about? He works in a bodega."

My team had no litigator. None of us could really argue, least of all me. On the basketball court, I was mute, or what words I actually did say hardly count as language; a transcript, it occurs to me, would sound vaguely pornographic: "Yes, yes! That's right! Give it to me! Here! Come on!" For one thing, I refuse to say the word "nigga." This is an essential linguistic enzyme in the construction of sentences used for street-ball litigation. Other words rarely heard from me are "dog" and "son." It's always the white guys who use these words who end up wanting to fight me.

We played hard in our second game. Monsieur M! I loved him. His jump shot looked like a shotput, he would take two massive dribbles, lift off with both feet, and throw it in the direction of the rim, but the shot was falling. He was flowing. The Laughing Man rolled to the hoop, bruising everyone around him, and I had my rebounds and short jumpers. The game eked forward, a violent game of chess. Then Monsieur M unleashed a series of his funny jump shots, and we won. I wandered off, exultant. And then, for the first time since last fall, I saw Lana.

4.

Over the course of the autumn and winter, the outlook for the court's future had gone from bleak to cautiously sunny.

A meeting had been called by Community Board 2 to discuss the fate of the court. The day of the meeting was a spectacular Indian summer day, and the court was mobbed. Each of the three half-court baskets had two teams of four waiting to play, the full court was packed, and no one was paying any attention to the fliers about the meeting that had been taped here and there around the park.

But as six o'clock approached there was a giant mood swing. Some of the regulars said they were going, and at the last moment a large contingent of sweaty guys in shorts headed for a cramped room in an NYU building, where the meeting took place.

"It was immediately apparent that this was an incredible turnout for a Community Board Two Parks and Recreation Committee hearing, possibly the best-attended hearing the Committee had ever seen," a friend e-mailed afterward. The plan to privatize the court and resurface it was abandoned in the face of community opposition.

I TOLD Lana I was writing about the court, and that I refer to her in my piece as the Crazy Lady. "But in a good way."

She raised an eyebrow.

"You have to be careful with that," she said. "There really *are* a lot of crazy people in this city. We have the lady who feeds the pigeons, for example."

The subtext of Lana's remark seemed profound: How easy it is to write off someone who is fighting for some ideal as a crazy person—a crank or eccentric who is simply acting out her own issues.

"It's great that we seem to have won," I said.

"There are a lot of people who use this park," she said. "This park is important to a lot of people. They *need* this place."

As Lana and I chatted, I noticed the new hotel that was rapidly rising on a former parking lot across the street from the court. Some of the rooms will have a view of the meatpacking district, others of the West Village, and still others of Chelsea. Some guests will look out and see, right across the street, a big stretch of not-very-pretty asphalt on which people are jumping around in baggy shorts, playing basketball. If they see that, they'll know they're in New York.

It was a rosy dusk. The court cleared. I practiced some dunks. I bounced the ball in a trance, vowing to get skinny, to be strong, to move around the city and play at other courts, so that the whole fluctuating but familiar family of basketball junkies who go to Horatio Street don't get too familiar. I promised myself not to disappear too far down the rabbit hole of street basketball, walked in circles bouncing the ball, and took foul shots in the soft and almost gauzy darkening heat. I was wretched, sticky, dirty, thirsty, thrilled. Finally, I went home.

A BIKE MESSENGER IN THE CITY

★

38 years old

THERE ARE BUILDINGS IN NEW YORK THAT DO NOT exist. Take 200 East Forty-second Street, for example. I was sent there for a pickup on a foggy October morning. They were tearing up the asphalt on Forty-second Street. A layer of dust rose up to meet the foggy, thick air. The wheels of my bike jittered on the road's stubbly surface as I rolled past Grand Central Station. I had just made a harrowing pickup at 60 East Forty-second Street. That building has its own messenger center. You duck out of the lobby down a staircase and find yourself in a semi-public tunnel on the way to the subway. There are two battered doors with the word "Messenger" on them. I went through the wrong one; it was the in-house messenger service for a company in that building.

"Wrong door," barked the guy behind the desk, without looking up. A room full of bored eyes fixed on me.

For a messenger there is only one thing worse than not being able to find the place where you are supposed to deliver a package—not being able to find the place where you are supposed to pick it up. I stepped out of one door and into the other. It was the messenger center. It held my message.

My first pickup in hand, I headed for another one nearby. When you are a messenger you pick up and deliver. You get paid by delivery, so each gesture has the whiff of cash. You hear a little register chime whenever you handle one of these items. I was about to collect another little chime.

Two hundred East Forty-second Street, however, was not where it ought to have been.

IF you are bored with your job, there is one surefire way to improve matters: Take some time off, even a couple of days, and work as a bike messenger. If your cubicle is too small, if the hours are too long, if the boss is too psychotic and makes your days hell because she suspects you of being happy at home, if your underlings are too snotty, if you wonder what it is like elsewhere, spend some time as a bike messenger, where elsewhere is the only place you will be. You'll return to work realizing how great you really have it, how good the pay is, how warm the office is, how many nooks and crannies exist in the day for leisure and your own private time. Or, conversely, you'll never come back, because you will have seen some of the world outside and decide you want to stay in it. Somewhere on the spectrum of self-improvement, between cucumber facials and psychoanalysis, a new contender is due to emerge—call it bike messenger therapy. It combines going to the gym with a kind of urban version of Outward Bound.

That was my idea, at least, when I called Rob Koch, my old boss at Breakaway Courier, where I had worked briefly in the early nineties, and asked for a job.

"Of course I remember you," he said. "I promise to never touch the flesh of another human being."

"What?"

"That's what you said when I gave you the Safety and Respect for Pedestrians speech. 'I promise to never touch the flesh of another human being.' I'll never forget it. So what can I do for you? You want a job?" Here he laughed for a while, until he realized he was laughing into silence. "Noool" he said. "What happened to the short stories? The journalism?"

I explained that I had long held the fantasy that if I didn't seem to be appreciating the opportunities I had, if I felt I wasn't applying myself enough, I would make myself be a bike messenger for a while to see if it changed my perspective.

"I had the exact same idea!" he said. "I wanted every company to give me their fattest, laziest, most overpaid employee, and I would put them through a kind of bike messenger boot camp for a week. It would shape them up. And the companies would pay me a fee. Plus I would get the messenger work for free!"

So far the idea had not caught on.

I visited Rob Koch in his office on West Thirty-fifth Street. When I last saw him, he was a gaunt man in a track suit and a beard, possessed of that utterly lean body that you see on professional bike racers like Lance Armstrong. He had been a messenger himself once, and when he started Breakaway he hired a single employee to dispatch the calls and did the deliveries himself. Now he has a crew cut, no beard, his face is rounder, and there are pictures of little children on his desk. His office is spacious and, as decor goes, a bit cold. There is a view of a sea of cubicles where his dispatchers huddle over computers, phones pressed to their ears all day like bond traders. Otherwise the main thing I notice upon entering are two mouse traps set in opposite corners of the room, each sporting a big hunk of cheese.

Breakaway Courier is now a big-time player in the messenger business, but they barely survived the dot-com boom when publicly underwritten companies like Kozmo and Urban Fetch threatened to put them out of business.

"There was so much Arrayan talk going on back then," he said.

"Aryan?" I said, wondering if in addition to the many sins of the dot-com era, there had been some sort of overt component of fascism.

"*Arrogant* talk. 'We're the future, you're history,' that kind of thing."

In addition to the dot-commers, Wall Street has, improbably, gotten into the bike messenger business, underwriting several giant consolidations. Of the four mammoth companies Wall Street underwrote, buying up mom-and-pop-size operations like Breakaway, three have gone out of business. Breakaway has been on a buying spree of its own, acquiring fifteen messenger services since 1988, though business is still touch and go, and nowhere near the levels before September 11, 2001.

Nevertheless, Rob tells me I can have a job, provided I go

through the Safety and Respect for Pedestrians talk, which is now a formal two-hour class complete with final exam.

"I'm not going to be a reliable, full-time worker," I tell him.

"That's all right," he says. "It's like in *Tropic of Capricorn*, when Henry Miller talks about being a dispatcher, and how you have your core messengers and your driftwood."

We discuss Miller's philosophizing about the messenger business and we stand up and shake hands, with the agreement that I am going to be driftwood.

ACCORDING to Noah Budnick of Transportation Alternatives, bike messengers have been around for about a hundred years. Their numbers in New York began to dwindle in the 1930s as the use of cars became more prevalent. But with the ensuing traffic congestion, the practice revived starting in the late sixties and boomed after the subway strike of 1980. In recent years the increasingly electronic nature of business has thinned their numbers somewhat, but at the same time bike messengers have become a global phenomenon. There are bike messengers plying their trade on topographies as disparate at Los Angeles, Washington, D.C., Denver, and Chicago. There is even a Breakaway office in Paris. I can't help thinking of the activity's ideal environment being Manhattan, partly out of sheer provincialism, I admit, but also because it is a vocation whose essence is navigating density.

Budnick estimates that there are around five thousand active bike messengers working in the city. I set off on my first delivery, making it five thousand and one.

★ ★ ★

OUT in the city things are happening all the time, as individual and numerous as whitecaps on the ocean, and for the most part as out of sight. As a bike messenger, you see them. In fact, there is something vaguely nautical about the activity, as though Manhattan were a giant ship over which you scamper in and out of small trapdoors and up masts, helping to keep the whole thing afloat. When you are a messenger, you are in transition. Therefore you see a lot of people in a similar mode, stepping out of one life and into another.

You see the young man in a bright red shirt, matching baseball cap, and baggy jeans, his beard trimmed to the width of an eyebrow running along his jaw, pausing outside a building to remove a blue button-down shirt from his bag, which he slips on with the sly air of a hip-hop Mr. Rogers putting on his work costume. You see the solitary elevator man smoking a cigar at 315 East Ninety-first Street relaxing in his elevator with a radio on.

At the St. Davies School on Eighty-ninth Street between Madison and Fifth Avenue, where the kids wear blazers and a nervous father jiggles his tasseled loafer as he waits outside the school office, there is a poster on the front door announcing an upcoming lecture: "Loving Without Spoiling."

I picked up at St. Davies and delivered to the GM Building, where they don't let messengers upstairs and there is no messenger center. The lobby of that building is a sea of lost souls holding a sandwich or an envelope, scanning the arrivals from the elevator banks, looking for a person whose face they have never seen.

You see the bottom tip of Manhattan, where new condos and grand hotels are springing up south of Ground Zero. The Ritz-Carlton at 10 West Street has a great lobby, but messengers are directed around the corner to "the gray door." Around the corner is a battalion of identical gray doors, each with a camera pointing down at the hapless messenger, who goes from one door to the next, looking for the nonexistent buzzer.

At three-fifteen in the afternoon, the waiting room at Abrams Talent, at 275 Seventh Avenue, looks like a day-care center or the waiting room of a pediatrician. Small children sit next to their parents, boys and girls and mothers and fathers in equal number.

"Does Abrams specialize in kiddie talent?" I ask a woman walking in with a cup of coffee.

"No," she says. "It's just that time of day."

All over town one sees the bright orange rectangles of parking tickets. Some are on the street. These discarded tickets pose an existential statement, gone today, drowning in the gutter, but certain to return in another, even more expensive form. Then there are the tickets stuck on the windshields of vans and trucks in motion. Do the owners leave them under the windshield wiper out of spite, or out of a kind of superstition that they will inoculate against any more tickets?

In the elevator at Forty-fourth Street and Sixth Avenue, a bald black man wears a giant green Buddha made of jade dangling from a necklace, and discusses office politics with an another man in the elevator. They each have a Dunkin Donuts coffee in their hand, large.

"Do you kiss up to your boss, is what all this comes down to," he says. "That is the question." The elevator is quiet for a moment. Then he answers the question. "Hell, no! You quit before you do that."

Bike messengers and writers have a lot in common, I discover. In both practices, every forward motion is self-propelled. If you stop trying, you will shortly stop moving, and stop earning. Both activities involve gathering things and dispersing them. Bike messengers are given specific destinations. Sometimes writers have specific destinations in mind, too. In both cases, however, how you get there is for you to figure out.

LOOKING for 200 East Forty-second Street, I biked east, past 150 East Forty-second Street, which stretched all the way to Third Avenue. Across Third Avenue was the Helmsley Hotel, 211 East Forty-second Street, which is the skyscraper version of a really shiny black car with black tinted windows and chrome hubcaps.

Back across Third Avenue, to 150. Then back one more time to Third Avenue. An entire building was not where it should be. It was my second day of work. When I used my two-way pager to communicate with the dispatcher, I had been instructed to use my courier ID number, "until I get used to you," he had said.

I considered how it would sound: "This is B521 here. I can't find my building."

I went back to 150, locked my bike, and entered the lobby. Later, I would find out some facts about this building—that it was originally called the Socony Mobile Building, that Socony stands for Standard Oil of New York, that it was built in 1956, that it was designed by the firm Harrison and Abromovitz and

Harris to serve as company headquarters, and that it is now owned by a secretive Japanese family named Hiro. But none of that will tell you what it was like to walk into the giant white-ness of the lobby, its marble floors so solid beneath my feet as to make me almost weightless in my anxiety about my lost building.

Looking for 200, I went into 150. I headed to the front desk, which was a good distance away, and above which hung a huge painting, a colorful abstract that somehow managed to convey a vaguely United Nations feeling, as though the small squares of color against a white canvas were all little flags. Behind the desk stood three neatly dressed black men arranged as though on a Motown album cover: red jackets, white shirts, well groomed, one sitting and the two standing on either side, each at a slight angle, facing toward the sitting man in the middle, the lead singer. They all turned in unison as I approached, like a dance move, a slight pivot. Their con-versation stopped. The movement was so subtle and well timed it seemed mechanical.

"I'm looking for 200 East Forty-second Street," I said.

"It's that way," said the man in the middle, and pointed east.

"But . . ."

"This is 150, so it's got to be that way," he said, and his eyes explained that was all he had to offer on the subject.

I turned and headed for the front door, and then, halfway across the lobby, which was curiously empty, I turned again to look at them and the giant painting above them. A single line from their resumed conversation drifted to me across the empty marble. It came from the lead singer, speaking to his two backups: "He only deals in cash."

★ ★ ★

I CAME out of 150 East Forty-second Street no closer to my destination of 200 East Forty-second Street and feeling very sorry for myself. I rolled down to Third Avenue and looked around, up and down the avenue. There I found my building, which is also 208 Third Avenue, between Forty-first and Forty-second Streets. The Third Avenue address is prominent, while the 200 East Forty-second Street is in small letters. The man in the lobby directed me to a special messenger entrance halfway around the block. The mystery of 200 West Forty-second Street was solved: It was on Forty-first Street.

STRIP CLUB

★

28 years old

I TOLD MY GIRLFRIEND I WAS GOING TO WRITE about strip clubs.

"When did you last go to one?" she asked.

"A few years ago," I said.

She gave me one of those long baleful stares whose meaning I can never be sure about, but which seem to suggest that she had suspected something really unpleasant and bad about me—had glimpsed it, or maybe its shadow—and now, like the Loch Ness Monster rising from the deep in all its hideous glory, it stood before her in plain sight.

"Come on," I said. "What's the big deal? It's practically wholesome!"

"It is *not* wholesome," she said, rather forcefully, and there the conversation ended, to my relief.

In the big picture, I was right. In the grand scheme of sex exploitation and violence voyeurism—in which hockey fights are spliced together to form one continuous face bash—a strip club is a harmless excursion, a night out with the boys.

But life is not lived in the big picture. It is lived moment to moment, and that first moment when one walks into a topless bar is not wholesome at all. You feel lust, relief, excitement, and revulsion. The revulsion, curiously, somehow enhances the other emotions. It's like jumping into the ocean—no matter how many times you've done it, you're never really quite prepared.

The shock of that first moment is the shock of the new. All day long you are surrounded by unknown breasts. They've been kept hidden behind bras and shirts, camouflaged by hunched shoulders, protected by crossed arms. You have seen skirts and shirts and you marvel that such thin layers of fabric are enough to cloak what lies beneath. But then you walk into a strip club and suddenly the curtain is lifted, the mystery revealed. Is this body exciting because of its own merit, or is it exciting because it doesn't belong to your girlfriend or wife?

It takes a second or a minute to adjust, but then, as with cold water or, more apropos, pornography, the shock wears off, and the naked woman onstage is just that—a woman who happens to be naked. The testosterone that brought you here diminishes, and it becomes just a place, a bar. That's the odd thing about strip clubs: the reason you go is not the reason you stay. Because strip clubs aren't just about women.

A FEW years ago, two friends and I sauntered into a place called Billy's Topless on Sixth Avenue. The atmosphere was no more illicit than if we had decided to get hamburgers. My friends were regulars. One was my age and the other, Nick, was an older man who reminded me of Dean Martin in his Rat Pack days—thin, stylish, and self-possessed.

My friend and I, the two junior members of the trio, looked up to Nick in a way, because he seemed to offer a solution to the conundrum of how to acknowledge one's more perverse, voracious, and generally seedy side, yet still seem like a gentleman and a decent human being. He could walk to the stage and slip a dollar bill into the hand of a dancer and smile at her with such debonair ease that when, several drinks into the evening, he professed that one dancer or another was in love with him, it was possible to believe him. Of course, he was a regular, so it was an ongoing relationship he was referring to. We could admire the guy, without necessarily wanting to be him. And so our evening had as much to do with Nick the diabetic drinker—he was now on club soda—as it did with the women onstage. Nick was elegant.

Strip clubs are often bastions of a kind of twisted chivalry. You see guys giving out dollar bills with a look of noblesse oblige. Sometimes they act as though they were presenting the stripper with a bouquet. More often it's a gesture of camaraderie: Yeah, thanks for the fun, baby, we all have jobs.

But this gesture is just an attempt to hold on to the self most people see out in the world. The moment you enter a topless bar you are woken from your civilized slumber and reminded of the style in which you want to fuck, and what a gross pig you can be. All the dormant, free-floating sexual aggression that has been hovering in the back of your mind all day, making little cameo appearances in your imagination at staggeringly inappropriate moments, now springs into action and takes over your whole brain. It's sort of a relief.

Most men manage to be gentlemen in a strip club, at least for a while. It's really a question of pride. You're in a strip club, but you don't want to seem desperate, even to yourself. But sooner or later comes that other incarnation, the lust-struck inebriate, who is the embodiment of a pathetic weakness to which everyone present can, on at least a tiny level, relate.

For every nine guys who seem under control, there is invariably one man with a craven expression of desire on his face, who wants dearly to engage this writhing creature onstage in the carnal scenarios he has been concocting while sitting at the bar. This man is not just having a good time drinking and collecting mental souvenirs to be used during some future sex fantasy—he wants to make it happen now. Really. You can see it on his face. This guy is not necessarily bad-looking, though at strip clubs, as at football and baseball games, you see some very ugly guys. There are always some amazingly pathetic-looking men in strip clubs—worshipful, bitter, ugly, and bent by the effects of too long without human contact. The impossibility of this contact, beyond the slight moment of handing over the dollar, makes the spectacle of their desire better and worse at the same time, by which I mean more interesting and also painful to watch.

The idea that the stripper actually likes you and thinks you're cute is a delusion I have veered precariously close to on a few occasions. Alcohol abets it a great deal. Most men get a bit sentimental and romantic when they get drunk. They want their lives to look pretty, to have architecture. With just a little wishful thinking, one is convinced that the naked woman onstage thinks you are attractive and wants to talk to you. The problem is that when you are drunk it can be hard to finesse these emotions. When drunk, you are like a recreational sailor who pilots his little Sunfish into the deep water for fun, but upon arriving is buffeted by severe winds. The waves are higher than you thought. You lose control.

One minute you're engaging in some harmless fantasy, and the next you are staggering up to the pulpit on which the strippers perform and handing over a dollar, your expression that of a deer blinded by headlights. One tries to be composed: Strippers are women, after all, and if you want to get to know them as women, as opposed to moving mannequins, you need to somehow get past this awkward situation in which you are pressing a dollar into their hand, or sliding it into the tiny strap of their G-string. So you make a joke, or say something sincere, something honest and flattering, and indulge in the high school fantasy that the class beauty will suddenly awake one morning and realize that you, among your whole class, are in fact the most desirable boy.

The stripper's response to this is to smile in a kind of sisterly, amused way, or to just playact at whatever role she wants to playact. Or, quite often, retreat into a tiny self-enclosed space of self-regard. These stages are always backed by mirrors, and they are more for the stripper's benefit, ultimately, than the patrons, who will actually try and avoid them, lest they catch a glimpse of that extremely unerotic sight: themselves. The mirror is the stripper's friend, and often the stripper will spend a lot of time staring into it, examining herself in a matter-of-fact, slightly curious way, watching herself dance.

This gaze is her statement of intent, as if to make it clear that the only person she really cares about pleasing is the one she sees in the mirror.

THERE used to be a seedy little topless bar downtown, across the street from a nursery (for plants, not kids). I'd drop by now and then after a long night out, sometimes with friends, sometimes without. Once, I was walking down the street with a friend and his girlfriend, and when we passed the place, she said she wanted to go in.

We were caught off guard. She explained she had never been inside one of these places, and she wanted to check it out and see what goes on. We made her promise that if she felt the slightest bit uncomfortable she would tell us and we would leave right away. When we walked in, I immediately started playing a video game by the door, my back to the stage, as if I couldn't bear to see what was there to be seen. My friend trailed after his girlfriend as she walked into the depths of the room to find a table. A minute into the game, my friend grabbed my arm, panicked.

"We have to leave right now," he said.

I turned, expecting to see his girlfriend in tow. But she wasn't there. He pointed down the length of the bar, where she sat beneath a gyrating stripper, her face as pale as the stripper's ass, and fixed in horror. She was having a bad trip, I could immediately see, and we had to grab her and evacuate. For the rest of the night she acted as if she had endured a brief bout of food poisoning.

I know there are some girls—strippers, for example—who don't find such environments a big deal, for whom a strip club has a certain noir charm. But even if my friend's girlfriend had been one of them—even if when we looked down the bar she had been sliding dollars into some girl's G-string and giving her ass a tart slap—we would have had to leave. The dynamic was all wrong. It was uncomfortable. This was not a place for girl-friends.

That's the paradoxical reality of strip clubs: The most fun to be had is with other guys. It's the last men's club. This place, where guys go for the explicit purpose of staring at bare asses and naked breasts, is one of the few remaining places men can go to not think about women.

A CAR
IS NOT
A CASTLE

★

39 years old

I ONCE MET AN ITALIAN WOMAN WHO TOLD ME about her castle. It was a real big old castle in the country. Her father had given it to her a few years earlier, and she was still trying to figure out if it was a gift or a punishment. Either way she was completely obsessed with keeping it from falling down. "Like a lover you should leave, but can't," is how she put it.

I own a green 1977 Thunderbird whose sunfaded, dilapidated elegance is an irrational source of pride. The car's condition is what I would call "appropriate for parking on New York City streets." It has two doors, opera windows, pinstripe tires, and looks as though the street might at any moment buckle under its weight.

I wouldn't call my car a lover, or a castle, for that matter, but I know how my Italian friend feels. Unlike her castle, however, my car was not passed down to me. It was not in the family for generations. Most importantly, unlike a castle, you cannot live in your car! (But this is not true, and the secret belief that if everything else went to hell I could live in the Thunderbird is probably the most unhealthy part of my attachment.)

The Thunderbird came to me, or I came to it, six years ago when I was contemplating a cross-country driving trip. I laid eyes on a behemoth from another age that looked like it would have difficulty making it down the block. It was a mystery car to which I am now, six years later, mysteriously attached.

BUT now it's time to say good-bye. By all rights it should be dead and gone, but like a character in some Stephen King story, it keeps coming back, or rather it refuses to leave.

This past summer, for example, the car broke down. In itself this is nothing new. It's been breaking down since the first week I owned it. But this past summer I rented a house on a steep hill that happened to be on top of a mountain. There was a dirt road, and the car was not happy going up and down. Its usual noises grew in sound and fury. Then one day it rolled to a stop on the side of a highway.

If you were driving by you would have witnessed a scene both bizarre and immediately understandable: A man stands on the steep embankment next to a woman, who is holding an umbrella to protect her from the sun. All around are charred rocks and weeds. It's the bland artificial nowheresville of America's highway roadsides. They always look strange when you see them standing still.

The man is now waving a pillow in front of the woman. Like a fan. Trying to cool the woman. At sixty miles an hour you would see the hulking mass of green steel sitting dormant, a spent volcano, you would see the man's slightly desperate chivalry with the waving pillow, and you would know the car would soon be history.

Unless the man is me.

I have been holding on to the car against reason for years. And so it was a shock when I took it to a small-town mechanic, an old-schooler, who I thought would be ideal to address this old-school car, and he told me to forget it. The car was beyond hope, he said, even though I had been able to drive the car, sputtering a bit, to his garage.

"It just doesn't have any more to give," he said.

"Why not?"

"It's old. You could put two thousand dollars into the engine and you wouldn't be done."

I was in a town three hours from home, and I asked what I should do if I wanted to drive back to the city.

"Buy a new car," he said.

"What do you suggest I do with this one?" I said.

"You could try and sell it."

"Who do you think would want to buy it?"

He thought about it for a moment.

"Maybe someone who needs parts."

MY relationship with this particular car began one spring six years ago, when I got it in my mind that I would spend the summer on a cross-country road trip by myself. I perused the classifieds, looking for the vehicle that would take me across the great land, and my eyes paused on a headline: "Starsky and Hutch."

The guy who owned it had recently moved from Minneapolis, where he had purchased it from someone else who had recently moved from LA. No salt, no rust, but the paint job was sun-faded, he said on the phone. We arranged to meet.

I got there early and scanned the block. The sun was an orange ball at the end of Twentieth Street, a burnt ember spotlight falling on a vehicle unlike any other around it. It had an almost feline weight and power, nimble but, bordering on sloth. And then there was the hood. Or should I say the nose? Because that is how I read it in that instant—a giant, majestic, overlong, preposterous nose. A Cyrano de Bergerac nose. A nose worthy of poetry and song. Massive, superfluous, impressive, strong. And you know what they say about cars with big noses.

Perhaps that nose reminded me of . . . me. Perhaps it was a bit like the one on my own face. Who knows why one falls in love? The car sat on Twentieth Street like a sleeping king, resting but poised.

"No, no!" a friend of mine yelled, jumping up and down like a madman the second he laid eyes on the car. "Don't do it! It'll drive you crazy!"

Another friend was amused at first but now thinks I am severely irrational. He has compared my persisting with this car to a teenage girl who runs to the bathroom after every meal. To this day, whenever the T-bird comes up in conversation, he puts a finger down his throat.

He's got a point. Owning a car like this, especially in New

York, where parking spaces have a value just below food and shelter, is irrational and a little self-destructive. But there is another way of looking at it, too. We all have our irrationalities. We all have our stubborn, obstinate, idiotic enthusiasms. And in the great pantheon of self-destructive acts, how bad is being overly attached to a stupid car?

The same friend who has taken to calling me a girl, for example, is unbelievably dysfunctional when it comes to women. He is a real connoisseur. He likes them blond and slender and a bit innocent, and though he talks about women a lot, and even sleeps with one of these perfect confections now and then, he has gone twenty years without the civilizing effects of a steady woman in his life. One senses his reason for this is that he is waiting for Gwyneth Paltrow to be single again. It's delusional. Compared to this sort of behavior, buying an old Thunderbird doesn't seem so bad.

The owner turned up. The car turned over. I drove it around the block. The power steering was graceful and smooth. Later that day I paid cash. I was its owner. I was thirty-three. It was my first car.

DOESN'T it drive you crazy to drive a car that is always on the verge of breaking down?" a friend of mine once asked. His was the most reasonable, accommodating voice. We were having an enjoyable night drive and the headlights had just blinked. It was an infinitesimal flicker, as though the car were about to express had suddenly vanished.

"Yeah," I said. "It does. But it's been running really well recently. And also, the good thing about worrying about your car is that it's just a car. You can fix a car. It takes your mind off of bigger, more important things, which you can't necessarily fix."

The car's headlights flickered again.

"It's like it lost its thought," I said.

"You're talking about it like it was a person," said my friend, laughing. We sat on the sofa that is the front seat and peered over the huge hood as we rolled down the road, enjoying the atmosphere.

The flicker of the headlights was the same imperceptible flicker that occurs when I'm introduced to someone at a party and, upon hearing their name, immediately forget it. It's the same flicker that men everywhere experience when they ask a stranger for driving directions, listen patiently, and then say thank you, only to realize that the entire speech has just been erased. We are the car. The car is us.

EVEN though the T-bird made it home, the mechanic's dour assessment drove me to extreme measures. I had to get rid of it. And so I summoned Todd Ashley. Ashley is an expert in the big monster muscle cars of the seventies. His company, Fast Ashley's, restores and sells them. Half his revenue comes from renting out the showroom for fashion shoots. The appeal of these late seventies American cars is far and wide. They somehow embody the whole spectrum of the American myth, from *Smokey and the Bandit* to Huggy Bear. Burt and Snoop. The cowboy hat and the velvet fedora.

My T-bird is solidly on the Huggy Bear end of things. Pimp My Ride would have a field day with it, but at the same time, it is a little redundant. For the '77 Thunderbird, pimping comes standard, factory-approved. Were it not for the sun-faded paint job and the ceiling fabric hanging down all over the place as though it were some kind of opium den, you could see Snoop Dog himself swinging open that giant door and placing a cream-colored shoe on the pavement.

Ashley is an Ohio native who now makes his home in Williamsburg; he's living in the land that made trucker hats an ironic style statement, and he's also a bit of a trucker. He's got that faraway, white-line fever look, five days past his last shave, faded blue jeans, and a Blackberry that is clearly his most trusted companion.

We meet at a café in front of which I have parked the car. Ashley is weary but indulgent, like a doctor going through the initial pleasantries of a house call before inspecting a patient. He's been buying and selling cars since high school, and in a way I think of him as a kind of artist or a writer—he's turned his affliction into his vocation. A friend of mine passes, and he and Ashley turn out to have met. They both used to own 1972 Chargers, and exchange notes on how much the model has appreciated in value.

"I just sold one in California for seven thousand," Ashley remarks laconically. "And I never actually laid eyes on it."

I realize I am secretly hoping he is going to deliver some wonderful piece of news about my Thunderbird. It's like *Antiques Roadshow*, but for cars. "Hey, Mr. Ashley, is this piece of junk actually a priceless work of art, or at least worth more than its weight in scrap?"

The answer is no. He breaks it to me softly, making appreciative noises as he looks it over. Then he points out that to really restore the body would cost about six thousand. And that's just the body.

"It's just hard to let go," I say.

"Letting go is good," says Ashley.

LETTING go is good! A bombshell!

I am really moved. I look at him with the wide eyes of a seeker, like I've arrived at some Tibetan mountaintop and been handed the key, the essential nugget.

"Yeah, I know, it's probably time to move on," I say.

"Right?"

"How long have you had it?"

"Six years."

"Six years! Oh, yeah, time to let go."

And here I involuntarily hold forth on the sensitive issue of women and the car. The fact, at once innocent and sordid, is that there has been more than one woman who has ridden shotgun in that car for substantial periods of time. And the woman who now rides shotgun, the one on the side of the road, the one I was fanning with the pillow—she is the last of the line, there won't be any more successors. I was in it for the long haul with her, and had recently announced my intentions. To her credit, her yes was not contingent on my getting rid of the car.

"So it's probably a good time for a change," I said.

"Oh, yeah," said Ashley. "You have to get a new car for a new girlfriend."

I once noticed, looking at the correlation between the novelist Saul Bellow's literary output and his marital history, that the man seemed to go through about one wife per novel. Ashley seemed to apply this principle to cars.

So it is all settled. Letting go is good! I'm going to let go. Just then a guy walking a little dog stops and says, "Hey, is that your car? I love this car! Whenever I see it parked here it just puts me in a good mood."

"Thank you," I say.

"Why don't you just give it to him?" says Ashley. "Just hand him the title right now."

I stammer at this suggestion. Take the leap, I think. Be bold! But before I can say anything, the guy with the little dog shakes his head.

"I couldn't take it. You can't have a car like this in the city without some serious resources."

He goes on for a while about his fond memories of his family's '78 Thunderbird, and the whole time I am thinking that even if I wanted to, I couldn't give the thing away.

Letting go might be good, but it isn't simple.

AFTER I bought the car, I had a honeymoon of about a week. I was starting to see a woman at the time, and I took her on a drive to a lake about forty minutes outside of New York. I knew about this place because, when I was little, it was where my mom would take me to practice driving. There was a big abandoned restaurant next to the lake, and I would tool around in that parking lot, giddily driving in circles. I have always loved to drive. Now I returned to this scene of formative steering in exultant triumph, driving a giant Thunderbird. We parked, so to speak. Then I made her sit on the car and I took pictures. In hindsight I can say I was behaving with the ridiculous enthusiasm of someone on safari in some earlier, more blithe moment in time, when you shot elephants without guilt and happily photographed your friends standing beside them.

I mention this because I have always wondered about the drug this car provides; I've noticed the high that registers on people's faces when they stop to look at it. I suppose I was having my first real dose of it that day.

After the little photo shoot we drove up the highway and this woman, this new person, laid her head down in my lap and fell asleep. I tried to position my arms so that they cast a shadow over her eyes.

SHORTLY after that, the car betrayed me. I was driving to meet this same woman in the country. Some friends had lent her their house. It was late, and I was on my way to paradise. Something went wrong. There was smoke, steam. I met the first of a long line of tow truck drivers. I could write a book about tow truck drivers at this point, or willingly read one by one of them. They are the pirates of the interstate, the ultimate ambulance chasers, and therefore a bit sinister. But they are also first responders coming to your aid. It's such a fraught little scene, riding in the front seat next to their stuff, listening to their radio station, full of the complicated feelings of the rescued and the rescuer.

I have fond memories of some of my earlier encounters—hats off to old Bing Randall up in Greenfield, Mass.! He assessed the damage in his garage and, having given me the terrible news that I had blown a head gasket (and a thousand dollars), drove me to the nearest Howard Johnson's and waited to make sure they had a room. They did not; and so I spent the night in their conference room on a cot, where I lay in the dark smelling the old stale smell of coffee and trying to take consolation from the sliding metal sign on the front door: "The Meeting Is In/Out of Session," it read. You could slide a piece of metal back and forth to indicate In or Out. I snapped crisply to In, and then went and lay in a big empty space in the dark.

Then there was the glassy-eyed guy with a gigantic paunch who showed up on Washington Street, blocks from my own house. His name was Dick and he had that clean-cut rebel look, like a biker from the fifties. He brightened when he saw the car. He had the word "Dick" tattooed in old blue ink on his neck, and looked like he had once been lean and mean but had since gone on a liquid diet of Budweiser for twenty years, a kind of anti-Atkins special, all carbs all the time. He told me about his old Thunderbird, just like mine, and in so doing introduced me to the weird duality of logic I would subsequently encounter in a lot of owners of the '77 and '78 model Thunderbirds: "It was the favorite car I ever drove," he said, "but I got rid of it because it was a piece of shit."

THE summer before my road trip with the T-bird I had taken a cross-country trip with my girlfriend at the time. We drove a very spiffy Jeep that belonged to her father. I had this nagging feeling that I didn't want to be with this woman and the fact that I was driving her father's car taunted me. It was a fun trip, but I was already planning my escape from that relationship.

So this time I was going to do it right, in my own car, where I could play the music as loud as I wanted.

After that initial breakdown, the one where courtly Bing Randall took me to Howard Johnson's in Greenfield, the car flew across the country. It was like driving the space shuttle through the American vastness. It took me up through the spooky and beautiful landscape of Route 12 in Montana, and down through Utah's national parks. It climbed the Rockies. I was alone for all this, and so, in the long tradition of men driving alone cross-country, I went a little crazy.

There was that lonely sunstruck stretch of highway in North Dakota, coming into Bismarck, when, as an experiment, I jerked off at eighty miles per hour. A few hours later I was gambling at a bar. You can do that in North Dakota, the bars all have little blackjack tables, and they even take personal checks, which I think is cruel. It was me and three guys from the North Dakota State University campus up the road; they were state troopers taking courses to get a leg up in the system. Me, two Indians, and a white guy with a mustache. One of the Indians was losing so much money, writing check after check. We all bought each other drinks, made friends, talked.

There is something about seeing someone lose money, or even losing money with him, that is bonding. The Clinton saga was unfolding on the TV, so our bets took place against a backdrop of shouts like, "If only you would have given him a blow job, Hillary, this never would have happened!"

Finally, the big Indian was broke. We were all very drunk. I stood up, and he looked at my T-shirt.

"You played ball in Brooklyn?"

Indeed I did, and my St. Ann's Steamers basketball T-shirt

said so. He played basketball, too, and we traded stories, and then somehow we decided to trade shirts. So all of a sudden we're taking off our shirts, and signing each other's shirts with a Sharpie as though we were all-stars. His shirt said "Four Bears Casino." His friend signed it, "Chief Dunk-A-Lunk."

I signed my shirt and stepped back. Then, and only then, did the horror of my earlier experience in autoerotic driving come back to me, when I saw the terrible stain. I have felt guilty for that ever since, and wish they stopped taking personal checks at those little mini-casinos outside of Bismarck, and cherished my "Four Bears Casino" shirt, signed by the two Indians who were state troopers and basketball stars in their recent youth.

None of this was a direct result of my owning a Thunderbird. It could have been a Corolla I staggered out to in the parking lot, really. But it was not. It was this giant thing that I guided down the road for a while, turning onto progressively smaller roads until I felt I was safely in the middle of nowhere. Then I curled up on the long front seat, a couch, a living room with wheels. And I slept. When I woke, I found my intuition was right. I was in the middle of a greater, bigger, vaster emptiness than I had ever seen with my own eyes, excluding the ocean. My heart filled. I felt like my chosen destination—nowhere.

From there, it was only another three thousand or so miles till home.

A FEW years later, on a road trip through Cape Cod, I made an impromptu stop at the summer camp I went to years ago. It's an old snappish sailing camp that has been around forever. I was given a tour. All the old cabins were still there. I was told that for at least a decade there had been a "no graffiti" rule in effect, and so when I got to one of my old cabins, the scribbles up there on the ceiling had the feel of an archive. I looked around and then my heart jumped. There above the top bunk was my name drawn in thick block letters, in pencil. Beneath it was a number: '77. I must have gone through a whole pencil writing that out, such was the fanatic intensity of the scrawl. Part of me recognized the sheer authorial vanity of a writer in that graffiti, and another part of me was simply stunned to think that the year I wrote that was the year a car was made that would take me back to this place twenty-five years later.

PROUST'S great memory stimulant was a cookie, but for a lot of people, automobiles fill that role. That, at least, is the only explanation for why people look at the car the way they do.

The 1977 Thunderbird is a car that, it turns out, a lot of people remember from their childhood. It is known as the last of the big birds, and it was, along with its successor model in 1978, a huge hit. Shortly thereafter the times changed, the design changed, and the Thunderbird model began its slow slide to oblivion.

"We had that car when I was a kid," I've heard people say. "My dad loved that car."

But a lot of people love this car for some irrational reason that goes beyond a personal connection. It feels like the end of an era. Its size, the weird conflation of sportiness and leisure, the opera windows—it all has an imperial vibe, but it's the atmosphere of a lost empire, or a lost innocence. Then again, you could argue that what it represents is a moment when Detroit had lost its mind. What were they thinking, putting out this behemoth three years after the oil shocks? And here I am, in another post-oil-shock moment, with a car that does to a forty-dollar tank of gas what magicians are famous for doing to ladies with their black boxes. It's delusional. But the element of delusion is romantic, too. It's as though the car itself were a kind of Don Quixote, its huge imperial nose always tilting at windmills, but ending up on the side of the road, waiting for a tow.

WALKING

THE

DOG

★

22 years old

MANY YEARS LATER I SAW HER AT A PARTY. WE practically bumped into one another in the dark. She recognized me right away. We both blurted out: "Oh-my-God! What are you doing here?"

I was visiting a small European city with my girlfriend, Elizabeth. The invitation to the party had come through a friend of a friend, whom I had only spoken to on the phone. I had expected a sea of strangers, which was what we encountered, at first. Suddenly the wife of my old employer loomed before us. I introduced her to Elizabeth. She introduced me to the man standing beside her. He had a beard, wine-stained lips, and a kind face. There was no mistaking him for her husband, my old boss. In the course of these introductions, we tried to explain how we knew each other. It came out in fragments.

"From a long time ago," I said to Elizabeth.

"We shared a kind of moment," she said.

"I worked for . . . her husband. An artist."

"It was . . ."

"Eventful."

"You can never write about that!" she practically screamed.

1.

I once wanted to be an art dealer. For two summers during college I worked for art galleries in Soho. I was interested in art, and in money, but I think it may have been the sandwiches at Dean & DeLuca, and the way the light fell in a place called "Food" on Prince Street, and the lonely cobblestone streets of that neighborhood that influenced me as much as anything. Soho then was populated by paint-speckled idealists, dazed from work in their lofts, who came out to stand on street corners and watch a parade of their own invention that was passing them by.

Looking back, it seems hard to believe that I wasted my time with this brief infatuation, but you can't punish yourself for your past ambitions, there is no point, and I did get an education of sorts, even if it was an education in humiliation above all else. I suppose it is inevitable that somewhere in the intersection of art and money there will always be humiliation; art isn't a necessary ingredient, but it raises the emotional stakes and makes you more vulnerable.

★ ★ ★

MY first job was at the Leo Castelli Gallery. Its shows of gallery artists like Jasper Johns, Andy Warhol, Roy Lichtenstein, Ellsworth Kelly, and Robert Rauschenberg made it feel less like a gallery and more like a very small museum. I was hired by an incredibly handsome, charismatic man named Tom MacGregor, who was in charge of the physical operations of the gallery—the job's official title was "preparator."

I liked that word; I felt it held a faint implication that I would somehow be getting prepared.

MacGregor had told me again and again, over the phone and in person, that there was no job, but I persisted and he finally hired me for a special project. The project was in the basement, where various crates had been moldering for nearly twenty years. All sorts of important artworks were in those crates. But no one knew exactly what was where in that dark, low-ceilinged space. I was hired to be a kind of an art mole, burrowing through the dank space with a crowbar. Periodically I came upstairs with progress reports. Strange metal globs were in one crate. A fluorescent light in another. The news was always greeted with excitement. Apparently it was all treasure.

WHEN the task was mostly completed, the crates opened, cataloged, and restacked with labels, Tom MacGregor agreed to keep me on as a kind of house schlep, and I moved upstairs. I now had lunch in the wonderful world of the gallery girls who sat in the room behind the front desk. Eventually I even got to help them in organizing the gallery archives. This was my education in contemporary art. I also helped open the mail, which led to a different kind of education. Leo Castelli was a dapper, dainty, vigorous man in his late seventies. He was past his club-going years—so I thought—and therefore he had no need for all the invitations he received to Area, the Palladium, and other nightclubs, which I took for myself.

The Castelli Gallery was a friendly place. Most of the staff, including a pair of sisters, had a kind of midwestern wholesomeness and, to my uneducated eyes, seemed to lack the guile and cunning I presumed was necessary to survive in the cut-throat art world. Only Leo, with his natty, neatly tailored suits, his quick eyes, his atmosphere of extremely refined libido, gave a sense that he could defend the gallery in the viperish world in which he had achieved so much. Many years later, the whole friendly gallery gang, a kind of family, was abruptly uprooted when Leo married a much younger woman who quickly maneuvered to separate him from his loyal staff, and I was reminded of that initial sense of vulnerability in everyone there but Leo.

THE next summer I worked at the Paula Cooper Gallery, another distinguished Soho gallery, again in the basement, though in this case it was a clean, well-lit basement where the tools, the brooms, the packing equipment, and so forth were situated. There was a doorway at the top of the stairs that led down to the basement, and it made a banging noise whenever it was opened.

For a month I took it easy when alone in the basement, often on the phone to my friend Tom Cushman, but whenever I heard the bang of that door opening, I got busy. One day I heard the bang. Cushman was saying something interesting. I decided to stay on the phone. It was the wrong move, and that was the last day of my job. But I left with absolutely no acrimony, no hard feelings at all, it was fair, I wasn't good at the tasks they hired me for and I wasn't working hard, and school was just a month away. My interest in being an art dealer had by then evaporated.

Those were the summers of close calls. I was happy for these interesting, slightly glamorous, not-too-bad-paying summer jobs. The only problem was that the actual tasks required a precision of movement, a handiness, that I did not posses. I was a bit of a klutz. I had moved, polished, hung, packed, and nearly dropped work by Warhol, Frank Stella, Donald Judd, Carl Andre, Dan Flavin, Ellsworth Kelly, Elizabeth Murray, Jennifer Bartlett, Joel Shapiro, and many others.

I had gotten under a giant piece of colorful canvas with its maker, Claes Oldenburg, and the two of us wrestled with it like kids under a tarp until we got it packed away properly. I polished a Donald Judd box with Noxon for three straight days. I spent time in the storage area a few floors above the gallery, lounging on a sea of Carl Andre's wooden railroad ties. I traced Bruce Nauman's obscene, life-sized clown figures so his original drawings could be spared being sent to the neon fabricator. It was an intense, hypnotic way to interact with artwork one would otherwise see on the wall, probably at a museum. It was fun. And it was an education in both art and art's relationship to money. I had peered at a fluorescent tube in awe, not of its beauty, but because I had just been told that this tube that I had been asked to polish with Windex, seemingly like any other fluorescent light, had a value of tens of thousands of dollars. It increased my sense of the value of art, literally, and it also made money itself seem like a kind of joke.

The creator of that fluorescent tube, Dan Flavin, was part of a group show at the Castelli Gallery the summer I worked there, and during that month he spent a lot of time hanging around in the back area. He was a portly guy in a Mets hat and flannel shirt. During the nineties there was a big revival of interest in his minimalist work, but the emotive eighties seemed to have put him in a bad mood. One day I was mopping the floor.

"Kid, let me show you how that is done," he said, and he took the mop from me and began to move it around in demonstration, with commentary. There was a huge sculpture sitting nearby, an oversized human figure poised in a position halfway between Rodin's *The Thinker* and a pose from the Mr. Universe competition. It was made by Sandro Chia. It had bright orange and yellow paint all over it.

"You have to put your back into it," said Flavin, demonstrating proper mopping technique, and here he splattered the sculpture with water from the mop. "You need to get into a rhythm," he said, and then he delivered a kind of Bruce Lee kick to the sculpture behind him, his work boot slapping against the sculpture's orange and yellow surface.

2.

By the time I left college a couple of years later, I knew I wanted to be a writer. But the jobs at those galleries were the jobs that I had.

While laconically looking for work that would sustain me while I did, or at least fantasized about, the work I was really going to do, I heard about an artist who was looking for an assistant. His studio had none of the messy, colorful accoutrement of painting. It was closer in spirit to an architect's work space. His office was at one end of his home, a long narrow loft with polished black floors. In the middle of the loft sat a pool table. My eyes lit up when I saw it.

The job interview was brief, our manner bemused. The Artist was a tall, lean man with long dark hair and wire-rimmed glasses that perched on a lean, angular face. He had a nose so small it looked as though it might be hard to breath through. He possessed a kind of tousled jolliness intercut with severity, generosity, sloth, intelligence, quick wits, and a short temper. On all grounds except the last one I thought it seemed a promising match. He already had an assistant who helped him with his art. I would do everything else.

MY job with the Artist began shortly after he married. The Artist's wife was quite a bit younger than he was, a graduate student, not more than a few years older than me. She had a round, open face, straight blond hair, and bangs. It was a Scandinavian face, a little doll-like. She was pretty, but her prettiness was colored by a faint aura of pleading around her eyes. I noticed it right away, and wondered vaguely what it was she might be pleading for. She seemed visibly excited about her new life even if she was maybe a little uncomfortable with her new role as mistress of the long, black-floored loft.

Looking back on it, it occurs to me that she moved through that loft with a giddy excitement that in an odd way resembled my own. Both of us were adjusting to a playgroundlike space where we would now be spending a lot of time.

She was immediately a difficult figure for me. I felt a kind of moral obligation to at least entertain thoughts about screwing my boss's much younger wife. But the feeling was not there, and I felt as though I had let the situation down. She belongs to a strange subset of experience in my life in which the sense of regret is not about what might have been—the affair or whatever—but rather that I failed to provide the spark of lust that would infuse the situation with, at the least, the drama of what might have been. Instead the Artist's wife occupied a zone closer to sibling; there was a faint undercurrent of competitive tension. I was not her peer, I worked for her husband and therefore for her, and yet there we were, both recently graduated from rather similar colleges, starting careers, roaming the expanse of that polished black floor.

AT the end of my first day my boss and I drank beers and played pool. I liked his quick, bellicose mind. The next day there may have been a few more games of pool. On the third day, during a midday lull, I racked up the balls and broke. I shot a few more balls and then the Artist came charging out of his office, black socks slipping on the shiny black floor, enraged. The sound of pool balls, I was told, drove him crazy during the day.

In this matter, and nearly every other, I feel I was in the wrong—you don't shoot pool on the job, at least not when the boss is there—however, I feel, given the context, the mistake was understandable. Somewhat. The lines between work and life, home and office, were blurry.

★ ★ ★

A LOT of my tasks fell under the general heading of "clearing out of his past life," that long party that he had wisely decided to end, he implied, before it ended him. I was at the fulcrum between the old and the new, the new being his wife.

One day she came upon me wrestling a box of magazines out from under her bed.

"What are you doing?"

"Uhm, it's the porn," I said, kneeling beside the bed. "I'm taking it out."

A long pause. "That's good."

"Out goes the porn," said the Artist wryly when I walked by holding the box. We all laughed. The porn was a comic relic of the past, as was the remarkably huge bindle of coke I discovered behind a bookshelf. She saw that, too, and remarked on it.

"It's gigantic!" she said.

"There were many piggy noses to feed," he said, and we all laughed again in a kind of mock conspiracy of homemaking. I opened it wondering if perhaps there was more left. It was empty. Its size impressed me. I was proud of my boss for the scale of his past frolicking.

Things got strange as I became more involved in the life of the household. She brought home giant dusters affixed to poles, and we both tried to use them to dust the ceiling fans. It didn't go too well. And then there was the vitamin C. The wife complained that I had eaten all the chewable vitamin C. It was true. It was one of those days. I had eaten all the chewable vitamin C. I went on a binge. I don't deny it. They tasted really good, like baby aspirin. The bottle was full in the morning, by the afternoon there were about three left. What was difficult was that she complained to him, and he berated me, and then I walked out of his office and there she was, a sibling who had won a round in an ongoing skirmish.

I MADE friends with the first assistant, Jay, an artist himself. He was an extremely wholesome and friendly guy from Indiana whose taste in sex veered toward picking up straight hustlers in bad neighborhoods. I worried about him, but he was so blithe as to seem indestructible. If his nights sounded out of control, by day he was a model of restraint and organization. I began to realize that Jay was part of a long line of artists who had worked for the Artist, many of whom had become well-known artists themselves. Jay was involved in an apprenticeship. But this didn't apply to me. I wanted to be a writer, not an artist. I remember talking about it with the Artist's wife once. She asked me, as I was helping carry something, what it was I really wanted to do. I felt grateful to her for her interest. But it also felt a little like chatting with a peer about our future plans. She was still in graduate school, just a few years older than me.

Weeks turned to months, and I became more wrapped up in the Artist's private domain. I received a small weekly check, and the vague intimation, almost Mafioso-like, of his future friendship and patronage, which would have mattered to me if I were an aspiring artist instead of an aspiring writer.

ONE day, I came across a Polaroid of the boss's wife naked. I flinched for a moment when I saw it. She was facing the camera, maybe walking toward it, wearing nothing but black stockings and garter belts. But her body was not nearly so naked as the expression on her face. It seemed on the verge of laughter, but also to contain a kind of plea directed at the photographer, whom I assumed was her husband. I wasn't sure what this plea was for, exactly. Maybe it was a plea to not leave this picture lying around where the assistants would see it.

I HAD a tendency to fail at small tasks. One chilly day I was sent out at lunchtime for two cheeseburgers and a *New York Post*. I did not return for two hours. The burger place was across the street on Broadway. And the *New York Post*? How hard could that be? As it happened, there was some sort of newspaper drought that day. I could not find a copy of the *New York Post*. All the boxes were empty. The newsstands were dry. I wandered the neighborhood with the cooling, then cold, then frozen burgers in ever-widening circles, and finally returned with the paper at three in the afternoon.

The tirade that ensued was ugly. I entered the office while he was yelling into the phone at some airline personnel, and when that was done he turned to me and my bag of frozen cheeseburgers and turned up the volume another notch. The scene was complicated by the fact that I empathized. He was being a jerk with his temper tantrum. But really, how hard was it to get a paper and cheeseburgers from across the street? His young wife tiptoed delicately around this situation and others like it. Was she averting her eyes from necessary dirty work, or out of relief that the person getting yelled at was me and not her? I reciprocated with a sibling's resentment; why wasn't she sticking up for me in the face of her husband's torrential moods?

THEN the artist got a puppy. Apparently he always had the same kind of dog, and the mourning period for the last one had elapsed. Now there was a new personality in the house, and I was elated. I happily accepted dog-walking duties. It was a relief to be away from the loft, and I liked the little guy. His name was Sigmund.

There was no doubt as to who this dog was named after. I had been faintly tempted to share my own odd relationship with Sigmund Freud. I was the son of one psychoanalyst, the grandson of another. Freud's disembodied face had loomed over me from the spines of many books in my house growing up, a stern, faintly beneficent, and slightly comic figure who I assumed was a distant relative. I didn't share any of this, though. There was a harshness to the Artist's temperament that made me want to keep my own private life away from him.

I bonded with Sigmund the puppy instead. He was a little dog with a jowly face and a tiny tail. We took walks through Soho. We took in the sights. Sigmund was a disobedient little guy, and I liked him for that. The walks were supposed to achieve a purpose they rarely achieved. He kept shitting on the floor. In turn, I took longer walks. It didn't help. We would return from our long leisurely walks and twenty minutes later there would be a brown pile on the immaculate black floor, above which the Artist or his wife would be howling. I'd shrug at the mysteries of puppydom and privately cheer him on. Go Sigmund!

★ ★ ★

ONE day the Artist and I walked to Williams-Sonoma on West Broadway. We took Sigmund. I was the one holding the leash. It was a choker leash, and the little guy strained forward, paws scrabbling on the pavement, in spite of the pressure around his neck. It was a nice brisk day and the Artist and I chatted in good spirits on the walk down. In the store, we separated and browsed. The Artist was fiddling with some brushed-steel soup ladles of different sizes when I heard a belching sound. I looked down. A small pile of something the size and color of a sea sponge sat before the puppy on the gray carpet.

"Oh, God, he threw up," I said.

The Artist ran over. "You have to pick it up!" he said. He stood there with the two big spoons in his hands.

"It's your dog!" I said. "You pick it up!"

"Clean it up!" he yelled, gesturing with the spoons.

It was a Marx Brothers routine. He waved the spoons. I stomped my feet. Sigmund sat there placidly, as though he had eaten a good lunch, as opposed to having just lost it. Finally a store employee came over and picked it up for us.

SIGMUND continued to shit on the floor. It was part of the daily ritual. He seemed to prefer the vicinity of the living room couch. Then one day I was instructed to use suppositories.

"You must be kidding," I said.

No, I was told, these wax suppositories would have the effect of forcing Sigmund to take a crap outside.

I held the box in my hand. They were pale, waxy things the

size of a rolled cigarette. "You want me to stick these up his ass?" I said. "No way!"

We had a standoff.

Sticking these waxy things in the puppy's butt would make him poop at the right time, I was told. At issue was my dignity, but also the dog's.

"It's a kind of violence!" I said.

But I did not have much ground to stand on. I could hardly be trusted to buy a cheeseburger and the paper. These were the duties left to me.

I suppose I should put all this to use in fiction, but it is too real to me: the sight of cold little Sigmund trembling on the sidewalk in the dark November rush hour while I tried to stick this waxy thing up his butt. The tight little knot of his ass clenched ferociously while he whimpered and I said, "I'm sorry! I'm sorry, Sigmund, this will only a take a second!"

I once announced to whoever was passing by, "I'm sticking something up Sigmund Freud's ass!"

What grand plans I once had for myself! I was now in charge of a specific part of a dog's anatomy. I watched somberly as Sigmund scampered around in discomfort with the little plug sticking out his butt until something came out. This went on for a while. At one point they ran out of suppositories and I was advised to use a match. I did. Sigmund, for his part, was not terribly fazed once he expelled the intruding object. He was a puppy. He was young. It was the only reality he knew. The big guy who took him on walks now punctuated them with this unpleasant insertion. Sometimes, after we went back upstairs, he still had enough left over to crap on the floor.

★　★　★

THE floor. The fucking floor. It was a totem, a philosophical treatise, and a statement of artistic intent to anyone who walked into the Artist's loft. It's blackness, smoothness, its sheer length, was the stage on which the drama of home and office took place, and it was the cause of the drama's finale.

Jay and I were hired by the Artist to refinish the floor. One day the Artist and his wife left on a trip to visit her parents, and while they were gone, a window of about four days, we were going to sand it down to bare wood and repaint it black. It was presented to us as a gift, an opportunity to log some serious hours, and before he left the Artist quipped that he always hired artists to do the job of skilled craftsmen, and it was usually a mistake.

"Then why do you keep doing it?" I asked.

"It's my generous nature," he said.

FOR three days we sanded. We wore masks. The machines had been rented from a place whose specialty was renting sanding machines. It was located just a few blocks away, a gritty reminder of the neighborhood's old character.

Sanding a wood floor is difficult. Especially when sanding a floor painted black, one is prone to falling into a kind of "Out out damned spot!" mind-set. You press the sander down until the black is gone, without thinking that the floor itself is made of wood, not marble or cement. Its smooth surface is highly perturbable. But . . . it was a war! No time to think abstractly. Dust everywhere. The place became a strange art installation of plastic tarp. One night I worked so late I simply slept there and woke up to continue sanding. I seriously contemplated sleeping in their bed. In the end I dragged some cushions onto a floor in the back. The Artist's quip about generosity was not entirely absurd; I was glad for the hours and fell asleep thinking of the cash.

The loft was in an old building whose side windows, like many in Soho and Tribeca, all had metal shutters. They were old and rusty, and they would sometimes bang in the wind. It created a huge racket on windy days, but the landlord would not remove them, in spite of the Artist's many pleas. I remember drifting into sleep that night and feeling strangely comforted by the sound of this banging.

I now know that the task of sanding a wood floor is a serious skill. You can't just press the sander down until the paint is gone. You have to keep it smooth. We didn't realize this important principle until we began to paint the floor. We got about twenty yards in and looked back. There was a surface worthy of a Jackson Pollock, if Pollock had worked in bas-relief, a black sea of squiggles, divots, and curves. It was the first time I ever saw Jay look worried. We finished painting the floor. There was nothing else to do.

When the Artist and his wife returned home, they brought us presents: hats and some moonshine. They came bustling in with their bags. Jay and I greeted them at the door. We stood there on the sculptural floor, ashamed, exhausted, and terrified. It took about five seconds for them to apprehend the damage. Then we all went to the living room and sat together in silence. I suppose Sigmund was there, but I don't remember what he was doing. We all wore hats. I held a bottle of moonshine.

It was a kind of wake. In a way, at that moment, the odd

subtext of family that haunted our arrangements came out in the open. We all sat as a group and grieved for the floor.

"I don't know if I should laugh or cry," said the Artist.

I WORKED for a few more weeks, then I quit, or was fired; it's hard to say. It was muddied by two concurrent strands of activity. One was a battle with the Artist to get paid for my work on the floor. The other was an interview with the Artist that I conducted for a magazine. He consented to the interview, and seemed to think I should be glad to leave it at that. But I wanted to get paid for the floor. Getting paid turned into a horrid battle. I'd put in about thirty hours on that floor, at seven dollars an hour. The Artist responded that he had to pay a specialist a huge sum to resand and repaint.

I told a friend about the situation. She worked for an artist showing at the same gallery as my boss. A strange kind of harassment ensued, in which my employer was mocked by her employer for being a cheapskate. I saw a note he sent, jeering my boss. The whole thing was really unpleasant. I felt like I had hired one part of the mob to pressure another part. More than a month after I quit I got a check with a nasty note.

About four months after I left the job for good, I found myself once more at the loft; I forgot why. It's possible I had been invited to a party; the line between abuse and friendliness was that fickle. Sigmund had grown and been fixed. He was lying in a pile on the floor when I walked in, but when he heard my voice he roused himself and ran over. He humped my leg joyously for a little while and then, perhaps his last rebellious act, for which I will always love him, he peed on the floor.

★ ★ ★

3.

I was on a Vespa, my girlfriend Elizabeth on the back, map in hand. When we finally arrived it felt as if we had navigated a maze. I was on assignment for a travel magazine, and my only task was to run around experiencing as much of the city as possible without giving a passing thought to cost. It was a glorious time.

We opened the front door and stepped into a brightly lit anteroom that was dominated by coats and a huge white basket of clementines still on the stem. Beyond that was a dark room full of people. We plunged in. I interrupted two people speaking in English and asked if they knew the woman who invited me. They did not. We moved on.

Then I came upon a person I recognized. We practically bumped into each other in the dark, and she recognized me right away. We both blurted out, "Oh my God! What are you doing here?"

She introduced me to her Italian boyfriend, and I introduced her to Elizabeth, adding that I knew this woman "from a long time ago."

"We shared a kind of moment," she said.

"I worked for . . . her husband. An artist."

"It was . . ."

"Eventful."

"You can never write about that!" she practically screamed.

"But you have hardly changed!" I said.

Was that true? She did look almost the same.

Come on, I thought, pull yourself together! No one is going to make you stick anything up a dog's ass! But you know, the horrible thing is that the safety net seems quite thin. No one is ever that far from walking the dog. You're either paralyzed with fear by this prospect or you use it to galvanize yourself to action, to the work you need to do. The tricky thing is that I say this in reference to one's artistic work, but accomplishment in that realm does not guarantee you won't have to walk the dog.

The Artist's wife spoke to me excitedly above the din. She informed me that she and her husband were now living in this town, a fact that depressed me a little, as I had that traveler's fantasy that the town was somehow my discovery, and now I had to deal with this unwelcome element. They had children. Then she told me she and her husband had separated.

"*You* know," she said.

I didn't know, but made a neutral kind of nodding gesture. I was in shock, really.

She said she loved him. She said he would always be the father of her children. "But," she said, "you know. He's just so *extreme!*"

She looked at me as though for commiseration.

Later on it occurred to me that sharing this remark might have been a sign of her loneliness; I don't mean that she was alone, but that her reasons for leaving her husband might have felt difficult to convey, and here was someone who might understand, even if she had not spoken to that someone in twenty years and hardly even knew him. At the time, though, I offered only blankness. Was I being discreet or withholding? A visceral memory surrounding the issue of this woman and boundaries visited me like a damp hand on my neck. Part of me wanted to extend myself. I wanted to feel a human warmth for her. I wanted to nod and say with knowingness that I did know, he could be extreme! But it was difficult. I looked at Elizabeth, who was smiling placidly, and her obliviousness to my history with this woman was a huge relief. It occurred to me that among other things, being with Elizabeth would mean that if I forgot who I was, she could remind me. There was no need to dwell. It was not, at any rate, *mandatory* that I explain, but this did not address the more central source of anxiety, which was that there really wasn't anything to explain. There was no affair, no profound exchange of thoughts or feelings, nothing, really, except maybe shame at my capacity for ineptitude, which, to Elizabeth's credit, probably wouldn't come as much of a surprise or be a deterrent to her affections.

We all stood there chatting for a few more minutes, and then we said good-bye with vague promises to see each other again. Then Elizabeth and I plunged back into the party searching for the woman who invited us, whom we never found.

LATER, Elizabeth and I were walking back to our Vespa in the dark. I was thinking about how the thing with parties is that the anticipation is often the best part. Then I saw the Artist's wife getting on the back of a Vespa. Her boyfriend gunned the engine just as she was fastening the strap of her helmet under her chin. Her head snapped back a little. She saw us then, and turned to wave, blond hair flying. She looked a little fragile. We waved back. The Vespa whipped around a corner, and then she was gone.

I thought about her blurted-out demand: *You can never write about that!*

It was a kind of inverted request, I thought. Maybe now, at the end of her marriage, she wanted me to write about what I witnessed at the beginning. If that sounds like an overly Freudian interpretation, let it be said that I had once been in charge of walking her husband's dog, whose name was Sigmund.

Then again, maybe she sincerely wished I never would write about it. Either way, it was an invitation. The obstacles that someone else puts in a writer's path are always gifts. You can now aim to surmount them, to defy them. They remind you of the singular freedom afforded by the act of writing. And they distract you from the much more troubling force field of gravity that emanates from within, invisible and binding.

We drove through the dark, quiet streets on our Vespa.

Elizabeth held on to me. The dark narrow streets with their old buildings rose up on either side of us. Total elation mingled around a knot in my chest. I was appalled to realize that my adrenaline was spurred in part by fear. Of what? Of embarrassing myself? Of some kind of retribution from the Artist—the memory of that old Mafia undertone? It's infuriating how the tormentors of your past are preserved in your imagination. On the bright side, though, I had an invitation. Or maybe it was a dare. *You can never write about that!* Either way, I knew I would take it up.

THE FLOATING ARMOIRE

★

39 years old

I HAD NEVER LIVED WITH ANYONE BEFORE. All the relationships I've had took place in a kind of extended apartment. If I were to map out these relationships, it would look like the flight plan for an airline. My apartment in the West Village is the hub, and there are routes to Tribeca, the East Village, Washington Square, and points beyond. Finally, there is a route to Gramercy Park, where Elizabeth lived in a very nice place with large windows.

I wanted things with Elizabeth to be new and different from anything that came before, and I had told her that. This new kind of relationship would be, among other things, one that continued. So one day I asked her to move in with me, in spite of the fact that she had the bigger place. My reason for this was the view out her windows. It was a view of a nondescript apartment building made out of sour brown brick. My windows looked over the tops of some Federal-era brownstones whose bricks were a reddish maroon, and the sky.

At first the significance of her moving in was largely conceptual. We already spent most of our time at my place. Her cat, Zoey, had been in residence for some time. And there were a couple of months left on her lease. Visits to Gramercy Park became exciting forays to some familiar but exotic hideout. At first, moving in meant moving a bunch more of her clothes. The battalion of little travel-sized bottles—creams, lotions, moisturizers—that had taken up position in my bathroom were replaced by their big big brothers. Still more clothes came over. We settled in happily to our new life.

There was one moment of hesitation on my part—it came after that excited moment of agreement when she said she would live with me. It was a single cloud in the blue sky of my thoughts. If she lives with me, said the cloud, it will be harder to end the relationship. I worried about this for a moment, until I remembered that I didn't want to end the relationship.

FOR nine months we had been engaged in a kind of electrical circuitry that by the day became bigger and more complex and more satisfying. It threw off sparks. It was exciting. Often it was shocking. Sometimes it overloaded and there was a black-out, and then the whole thing would have to come back online in parts, the vast grid of the city of us returning to light neighborhood by neighborhood, a ginger rebuilding, until it was again up to speed, whirring, blinking, and, like the universe, always expanding.

Elizabeth has a nice smile. It's a big American smile. Like most big smiles, it is on message in its smiliness, unambiguous. Sometimes, when she smiled at me, I'd feel this pang of infant joy that such a beautiful bright thing was directed at me. And then there was another look, almost the opposite of that smile, which fascinated me even more: her face in repose, unaware I was looking, or that anyone was looking. In that mode her face was some imperial dream from another epoch, another place in the past, and also the future. My future. Ours.

I loved that face. Maybe I loved its threat, the secrets it held, the feeling that she was a stranger. Who was she? She was the person I had asked to live with me. It was a union that anticipated other unions. We had discussed it. Our language often revolved around the word "forever." I was, in short, gearing myself up to propose. But I had a little trouble with the word "forever." It does not come naturally to me. Was it because I was not in love? No. Was it out of some superstition that once you start throwing words like "forever" around, you are inviting some sort of catastrophe? Maybe.

There was a period of time in my childhood when I had been obsessed by the strange overlap of meaning and mood between "forever," and "never." I talked about it a lot with my mother right before I fell asleep. Maybe it was after my father died, I don't remember. Those words were like two parallel roads leading into infinity, which was its own combination of forever and never. Or maybe they were not parallel and separate, exactly, but rather the edges of the same road—forever on your left, never on your right. And out in front of you stretches your life, all the way to the horizon. It tapers to a single point.

For me, the idea of marriage was always hovering somewhere between where I was and that single far-off point where forever and never merged. It floated in the realm of the possible, which is my favorite condition. There was a phrase attached to this condition when I was growing up: "something to look forward to."

My mother used this line when she had to undertake the disciplinary role in the household. It was how she softened the blow. When I couldn't do something I wanted or have something I wanted, she didn't leave it at that, she tried to show me the bright side. I couldn't have it now, she would say, but I could have it later. It was "something to look forward to."

THE time came to pack up Elizabeth's place. Forever. (Just practicing). The apartment, which had been dormant for months, sprang creakily to life on the occasion of its dismantling. Entering it, I was struck with a kind of vertigo of nostalgia. Here was a whole world of history that was about to vanish. She had lived in her place nearly as long as I had in mine, and there was close to a decade's worth of accumulation.

I have experience with the resilience of little things—buttons, postcards, pipe cleaners, key chains, eyeglasses whose tortoiseshell frames are so antiquated they seem cool, blue felt-tip pens whose ink, over time, fades from a sturdy dark blue to a kind of faint violet, like a watercolor sea. I'm speaking now of the little things of my father. I had grown up in an apartment that was, here and there, touched with the atmosphere of Pompeii. One's eye would move across a cluttered room and small details of my father, frozen in time, would emerge. A stray pipe. A pack of cigarettes—both Dunhills, which he smoked on special occasions, and which I tended to leave alone, and the more pedestrian Marlboroughs, which I would heedlessly steal by the pack and hide in an attempt to deprive him of his cigarettes. These little thefts inadvertently created little time capsules that would emerge years later during some cleaning out or rearranging of the apartment.

These objects were like the line of seashells and pebbles a wave makes when it washes onto the beach. They remain there long after the tide has gone out, a kind of algorithm of life, curving up and down. These mere things can form a kind of silhouette, collecting at the perimeter of where a person used to be.

There are now many more layers in that apartment. My mother has been single-handedly running a kind of scholarly center and movie production company out of the place for twenty years, and filing is not her strong suit. But not all the small things in that apartment are buried beneath layers. If I want to, I can revisit the small, smudgy handprints of my seven-year-old self, left on my parents' bedroom ceiling from when I had climbed up on the edge of a bedboard. The handprints can still be pointed out thirty-two years later, though the bed had since moved to the opposite wall, and the smudges now exist apart from the geometry of furniture that allowed them to appear in the first place. Drawers in that apartment are random archives. You don't just pull open a drawer to some side table. You avail yourself of a rarefied special collection, uncatalogued, of stray singular nothings of my father's stopped-in-midstride life. By which I mean he was fifty-two when he died of cancer. But I hate these blunt statistics. People always seek solace in the nonambiguity of numbers. And yet I met Elizabeth when I was around the same age that my father met my mother.

Now I felt that in a strange way he was back on the radar. For the first time since I was nine and had him in front of me, I could put my life alongside his. I knew what he was doing when he was my age. He was getting married! I could glimpse the concentric circles of generations, like the rings of a tree. I had *known* this all along, carried the image of those tree circles with me since grade school, but now I understood it a little bit, and in fathoming the distance between knowing and understanding, I acquired a little of that mystery and distance that kids always see on the faces of their parents.

WE entered her place, the petrified apartment. Some flowers I had bought her months earlier sat dried in a vase. The apartment creakily sprang to life on the occasion of its dismantling.

"We had so many great memories here!" I said.

"I know," she said, a little wistfully.

"And the place is so nice!" I said.

"Please," she said. She had a soft look on her face and gave a glance around the place, perhaps having doubts of her own.

"Don't start making me doubt whether we should be moving into this place instead of yours."

"Why not?" I said. "It's fun to doubt."

Damn it, I thought. Why? Why make it more complicated than it has to be? Why provoke?

"Not all the time," she said, and the ship sailed on.

I thought about all the fond memories this place held for us, and then I thought about all the fond memories that the place must hold for her, from before I even met her. She had lived here nearly nine years, all sorts of things had happened.

I knew of one boyfriend who had kicked down the front door in a rage, convinced she was with another man. She was alone, as it happened. And they had broken up anyway, so what right did he have? (And if they hadn't broken up? When is a locked door eligible for kicking in?) She had a lot more memories of the place than I did. Let's not appropriate what is not my own, I told myself. She seemed perfectly willing to get on with the business of getting on with things. Maybe her memories of the place weren't all so great.

And then a weird thing happened. I felt a pang of fondness for her bad memories.

BEING in her apartment was like time travel to our earliest days, when our activities were frantic and delirious. I was standing in the room I had stood in when she was still mostly a stranger to me, an unknown quantity, and my arrival had seemed a promising intrusion into her personal space that strongly suggested, but did not guarantee, other, more significant intrusions. And so in spite of her shouts that we had work to do, it was a long time before the first sweater was held up for examination.

This little siesta happened every time we went to her place to clean it out.

"It's the place, the special properties," I explained.

"It's that you have a natural aversion to work," she replied, clearly recalling many such siestas taken in lieu of many other projects. "You want to procrastinate as long as possible."

"It's the bed frame," I said. "It's a got a little, I don't know, something."

She did not dispute this. We agreed to take the bed frame to my place.

"WHAT about my armoire?" she said on the last visit before the movers came. It was wooden, heavy, big without being that spacious, and faintly gothic. The very choice of word "armoire" disarmed me. It hinted at the romantic, deeply hopeful side of her, the part that was capable of total joy and optimism. How could I deny her the armoire?

But! But it wouldn't look good in my place, which would soon be our place, I said. I would build her an armoire to replace it, I promised. Bigger, better, more beautiful.

A look of concern passed over her face. It wasn't ambivalence or indecision, exactly, more like doubt.

"What's the matter?" I said. I was tempted to add, "Don't you trust me?"

"I like my armoire," she said at last. "And I need a place for my clothes."

"I'm going to build you one that will be so much better than this one."

She looked at me and bit her lip.

"What?" I said.

"Well . . . I don't mean to suggest you aren't a good carpenter, but . . ."

"What about the bookshelves?" I yelled.

I had built some very basic bookshelves for my apartment to augment the ones I had dragged in from Shakespeare & Company, and I built a larger version of those very basic bookshelves for my office. In addition to the ones I built, there was a hand-built, nifty bookshelf that jutted out perpendicular to the wall which had lots of little architectural details. These, however, were designed and built by my upstairs neighbor, Hal, the architect.

The bookshelves I had built had various flaws. One was that I used nails and, as I was later told, "Screws are stronger." The other was that I had not banged the nails in all the way. I had left the heads protruding a tiny bit. It was a kind of commitmentphobia applied to carpentry. I thought it would be good if I had the option of being able to pull the nails out, should some calculation prove to be a mistake. The shelves sat there for years with these tiny protrusions. Shortly after I asked Elizabeth to move in, I noticed them and, decisively, banged them in all the way.

AND so it came to pass that we moved her clothes in big black garbage bags which were put under my desk, a temporary residence until I built her the glorious armoire. In hindsight, I may have sighed a little too relievedly at the end of that long day, when the last garbage bag of clothes had been stowed away.

The first step in building the armoire involved deciding where to put it and deciding on the dimensions, both of which we did together. So far, so good. Once we had the general idea, I visited Hal upstairs just to make sure I was on the right track.

Hal was an architect. He was about my age, a handsome, copper-haired man who for the eight years I had known him had been recovering from "the flood." He had arrived in our old, Federalist-era brownstone shortly before me. We had similar taste in music and literature, or at least we were both interested in music and literature. Hal, being a macho kind of aesthete, also collected first editions and had an enthusiasm for high-end stereo equipment that at times seemed a bit extreme. We were friends, but it was a neighbor thing. He had a zest for precision that, deep in my soul, I thought might be an impediment to emotional connection. Or, to put it another way, I thought the sooner he finished his renovation, the sooner he might have someone to enjoy it with. He, I suspect, may have secretly felt I lived in spiritual sloth.

MY first glimpse of Hal came after a night of heavy snow. I woke to the sound of scraping, a strange dreamlike sound at some ungodly hour near dawn. Irritated and curious, I peeked out the window to see a redheaded man shoveling snow off our steps with gusto. It was Hal. The way he shoveled the snow made it clear that this was a supremely pleasurable experience, a simple uncorrupted act before people showed up and turned everything to slush. There was an austerity to his spirit, I could tell. I found it admirable and have subsequently tried to make myself into a person who enjoys shoveling snow in the early morning hours. The transformation is not yet complete.

When Hal was not working the arduously long hours of an

architect, he was ceaselessly renovating his apartment on the top floor of our eccentric old brownstone. Technically, he was recovering from "the flood," but at the same point the renovation took on a life of its own. The flood had occurred just after his girlfriend of several years had moved out. I hardly had time to register her when I moved in. She was back briefly a couple of months later. I saw them through the plate-glass window of a restaurant in the neighborhood, sitting over a bottle of wine and holding hands. Then she was gone for good.

Shortly thereafter, the roof collapsed, and a torrential rain poured in while he was still at his office. For me, this event manifested itself as a water stain on the ceiling that was painted over. For Hal, the flood was a disaster of biblical proportions. He lost all his books—he had collected first editions of Borges and Calvino—and the furniture was ruined. And the floor. Most of his albums, too.

After the flood he turned his apartment into a cross between a construction site and an archaeological dig. It was the six-million-dollar-man principal applied to an apartment—we can rebuild it. Sleeker. Realer. Better! Old and new would exist in perfect calibration. I was periodically summoned upstairs to marvel at the discoveries and additions. The old gas meter in the bathroom had been stripped down to its bare, unpainted, original condition, for example; it was a lead box with a small window for the meter at its center; that little window onto the meter possessed a kind of faith in science that was touching and beautiful. I didn't ask how long it took to get the paint off.

His apartment consisted of perfectly restored details, a butcher-block counter for the kitchen, a hanging lamp from

Scandinavia, a Miro print, a leather chaise. The man had good taste. His place became beautiful. Then it became more beautiful. And still it remained a work in progress. The floor was covered in tarp, dust everywhere, tools on the table. Weekends I heard him rumbling around upstairs. This went on for years. Perhaps this is a curse that architects living in old buildings are particularly susceptible to. Or maybe it was something about Hal.

He kept architect hours. I'd hear his steps on the stairs when the morning light outside was still dim. He'd return late at night. And in his free time, he renovated.

He put in gorgeous shelves. And a new floor. The white walls were so dense and smooth they resembled walls of white butter. He built a skylight (or uncovered and rebuilt one that once existed). An antique harpsichord arrived (I helped carry it up the stairs), which, though he did not play it, looked extremely cool. There was also a vintage guitar. He had huge, wild parties, where musician friends jammed into the night.

There was a certain irrational, Dada-esque poetry to the renovation. We were renting, after all. One day he'd have to leave the gas meter behind.

I KNEW he had gone off the deep end when I emerged one Saturday morning to find him sitting on his staircase happily scraping away at the paint on the wooden banister with a tiny tool.

"What the hell is that?" I said, referring to the tool.

"Dentists use it," he said, beaming.

"You're kidding," I said.

"Isn't it gorgeous?" he said. "Cherrywood!"

I knew he meant both the old wood of the banister—which was seeing the light of day for the first time in at least fifty years—and the sheer artistic gesture of revealing it. I agreed, yes, both were gorgeous. But I worried for the guy.

I had to refrain from blurting out: "Stop building your place and start living in it!"

But he himself acknowledged this in jokes, and anyway, some truths can't be pointed out. Especially if they are being pointed out by a downstairs neighbor who, over a number of years, and several girlfriends, has often wondered about how much noise, how much sound, how much aural evidence of certain acts might be traveling up through the pipes and floorboards to the bedroom/showroom above.

ONE day Hal came down to my place when Elizabeth wasn't there and I showed him where I wanted to put the armoire. It was at the end of the bookshelf he had previously built with me, *for me*, really, about four years earlier, as a favor.

"You know what would be really cool," he said in a rapturous, murmurous mode. "If you built exactly what you described, but screwed it into the shelf behind it, so it floated."

I pictured it. I saw a beautiful piece of modern architecture floating off the ground in my own apartment. A pale birch box. It was like commissioning a small building, an autonomous structure.

"Yes!" I said. "That would be so cool! That would be so great! You're a genius! Yes!"

And thereby, in one heedless moment, I undertook a project

that was completely beyond my reach, a project that put me in the capable, but perhaps ever so slightly dysfunctional hands of Hal the Renovator. I had unwittingly consigned Elizabeth's wardrobe to purgatory, and in so doing commenced to send her a not entirely encouraging signal about my capacity for what lay before us on the road where never and forever converged.

TIME went by. Hal drew up plans with a list of every cut of wood we needed. Some more time went by as I put off going to the lumber store, which was in fact called "The Lumber Store." At some point I reached for the plans and they were not there. Had I lost them?

What followed was one of those terrible scenes when a grown man burrows into a desk drawer like a dog looking for a long-buried bone, stuff flying all over the place. Several convulsions of searches took place over the next couple of days. I was drifting into despair. Then the piece of paper materialized, like a well-hidden cat that had strolled out into the open, a relevant metaphor, since those same days had been punctuated by several panicked searches for Zoey the cat, who had a tendency to completely vanish into the seemingly finite space of the apartment. Losing the plans would not be nearly as bad as losing the cat. The panic of the pet owner whose beloved pet has disappeared is exceeded only by the panic of the person who loves the pet owner, and who may have to announce that he has somehow lost the prized pet.

The cat turned up; the plans turned up.

Then a lot of lumber turned up. It was beautiful, and I ran my hand over the smooth planes of birch plywood, marveling at the creamy, barely visible patterns in the wood, mysterious and organic. I thought all the wood would cheer her.

"When does all this wood trim turn into an armoire?" she asked.

"Soon," I said. "Any day now."

I refrained from telling her that the armoire was something to look forward to.

WHAT is it about carpentry that makes it so manly? There is the saintly, Jesus-like aspect of it, and the physical, nonverbal aspect of it; carpentry requires very little language. It mostly requires skill, concentration, an appreciation of geometry and gravity, and an eye toward longevity.

And yet why, when language is applied to carpentry, does it become a Pandora's box of puns? A Pandora's armoire! Every word associated with it is some kind of sexual noun/verb double entendre, starting with the material: Wood (the laying of). And: Nail. Screw. Hammer. Drill. Bang. Aggressive words, masculine words, a bit violent. These are not romantic words. Then there are words like "clamp," and "vise," landing us in a gray area, and then finally "saw," and "cut," which work in an entirely opposite direction, imagery-wise.

Beyond carpentry, the language of architecture is rich with metaphor. Hal's favorite architectural detail was something called a "remove." He used it in his large-scale architectural work as well as in little domestic contructions, including the bookshelf he had previously built for me.

A remove is a space that gives the illusion of lightness, such as when the space between a wall and a ceiling is punctuated by a small recess, as though the two are not actually connected. It's the architectural equivalent of white space on a page, an absence that is also a connection. It gives you the illusion of separation while maintaining a togetherness and interdependence. In architecture, and carpentry, it is a great thing. In a relationship, I'm not so sure. A lot of my relationships have taken place at a remove, literally. An ocean is a kind of remove, for example. So is a continent. So is someone's ambivalence, or grief. At a certain point, the extended apartment is a remove.

The floating armoire was an extreme case of a remove, and I wondered if that was an ideal state for something that had come to symbolize our togetherness.

Maybe I should have picked up on the sheer linguistic incongruity of it all. Wasn't the very word "remove" the opposite of what this moving-in thing was all about?

And was Hal—the renovator, workaholic, perfectionist—really the guy in whose hands I wanted to place my domestic bliss? A woman can tolerate her clothes in garbage bags under the desk for only a finite period of time. But I wasn't looking down and seeing those black garbage bags on the floor under my desk. I was looking up, to where my armoire would be floating.

NOW that the design had Hal's stamp, the work had to be deserving of the design. I signed on to a whole other view of the world, a view in which the angles were right, in which the lines were straight, in which form had equal billing with function, if not slightly higher. It was beyond my reach as a carpenter, and when Hal finally came down with some glue and a drill and some screws to begin the process, my role became that of a cheerleader and caterer. I opened beers, played records, chatted amiably. I learned. I asked questions. I watched closely. Sometimes I held a piece steady.

A few hours later a small but important amount of work had been done. "A step in the process," as Hal put it.

"Fantastic," I said. "Great!" And then I listened to Hal's steps ascend the stairs, a narrow gorgeous alley of white light that led to his single door. It was lined with a banister of lusciously dark cherrywood. I'd be lucky to see him again in a week. It could be two.

ELIZABETH came home that day and was not impressed. The place was now dominated by what looked like a half-built boat that reminded me faintly of a long-ago woodworking adventure at camp, when I undertook to build a cabinet for my first stereo. In the absence of the stereo's actual measurements, I calculated from memory, which is to say imagination. When some of the other kids looked at the gigantic structure I was at work on and asked me what it was, the shop instructor interjected, "It's his coffin if he doesn't finish it."

Although it was about ten times the size of my actual stereo, I finished the stereo cabinet. The same could not be said for the armoire.

Over a month had now passed since Elizabeth had moved in completely. Not only was she still living out of bags, but now there was wood all over the place. She worried that it might fall on the cat. She didn't quite come out and scream that she was living out of garbage bags in a lumberyard, but that was the direction things were heading.

And the odd thing was that it was Hal, in a sincere moment of friendship, who had offered me advice about living together. "People move in and think they've gotten past the hard part," he said. "But that's when things get difficult and you really have to work on it."

I thought, I'll work on the relationship! You work on the armoire! But I didn't say that. I went and popped another beer. It seemed to be the only thing I could do.

AND then it got ugly. I had long ago offered her all the space where my clothes were, which I would happily store under my desk, but she had refused. We were now firmly in the realm of symbolism, and all disputes that are symbolic are bound to be slightly doomed to violence, emotional or otherwise. She quoted various outside observers, friends of hers, who thought she was being eminently patient, if not downright saintly. She reminded me that I had convinced her not to bring her old armoire. The matter became urgent.

I WAS bugging Hal as much as I dared, but the man had a job, and besides, he was doing me a favor. I called some carpenters and, having described the job, was mortified to hear the size of this favor translated into dollar terms. I was about to bail on the beloved idea of the floating armoire and just slap it together when Hal appeared for another session. I had thought it would be so easy. And it had proved to be so hard. Except, voilà, the drill, the screws, the sawdust on the floor, the cat cowering in the corner, and there it was, done. A ship of clothes, floating in air.

HAL had some other ideas about the general perfecting of the thing, but he was happy to retreat back to his life. I showered him with thanks and a few weeks later he had knee surgery and I delivered ice and ginger ale to his door with a degree of missionary gusto that I think he recognized transcended mere friendship and neighborly courtesy and entered the realm of contrition.

Meanwhile, downstairs, Elizabeth and I and even the cat circled this new monument with delighted awe. The garbage bags were pulled out from under the desk and their contents carefully were transferred to the smooth spacious shelves. The two doors had been cut from the same piece of plywood and mounted on piano hinges. When closed, the delicate pattern of the grain ran across the cut, from one panel to the other. For a while it was as if we had moved into a whole new place, and in a way, we had.

I recalled a particularly stressful moment when Elizabeth, trying to explain the damaging aspects of the delayed armoire, used the metaphor of a cake that has been in the oven too long. What a domestic metaphor for a domestic predicament! I resented the duress I was being put under. I wanted it all to happen in its own time. First you build an armoire under pressure, and the next thing, you're getting married! It's not supposed to be under duress!

But why do I think that? Why do I think that point on the

horizon will always be out there, something to look forward to? Love, marriage . . . furniture-building—they are all formative experiences. And things are formed under pressure. Diamonds, for example. And the mountains surrounding us, for example, the geology of our molten earth, the movement of glaciers that cut valleys. Massive pressure! And they have been built to last, they are all still with us.

But maybe landscape is not the place one should look for parallels to human commitment. And anyway the armoire is made of wood, not the most permanent material. Also, it has occurred to me, we will one day have to leave our gorgeous spot. The kindly landlords who live downstairs and raised their family here are getting on in years. "They won't be here forever," I once said sadly to Elizabeth. And by extension, neither would we.

"But would you want to be here forever?" Elizabeth said when I shared this lament. She was looking forward, being practical.

"Well, if you think about it, we could cut a window in one of the armoire doors, and one of the shelves could make a very nice bassinet."

"Please tell me you are kidding," she said.
"Sort of," I said.

FOR a long time I left the armoire unfinished in one respect—the doors did not latch closed. The two planes of birch were so beautiful in the way their grain met at the cut, forming a cohesive single entity; I could have used interior magnets, but I didn't think they would be strong enough to keep the doors closed.

What they needed was a clasp on the front, but I didn't want to interrupt those smooth planes of wood. And so, three months after it went into action, when I pulled a diamond ring from my pocket, got down on a knee with flowers, and proposed, the armoire was still not entirely finished.

The events of that particular night were a bit random, my previous plans had been thrown off, and so I ended up popping the question in that very room. I took her by surprise, a surprise exacerbated by the fact that she turned around to find me down on one knee, holding a box with a diamond ring in it upside down.

I asked my question. She gasped, a sound I understood to mean happiness, but it was not quite a word.

"Was that a yes?" I said.

"Yes!" she said. "Yes!"

I stood, got the box turned the right way, and she slid the ring, which looked suitably dramatic, onto her finger. We embraced. The armoire floated nearby in all its splendor, its two doors slightly ajar.

ACKNOWLEDGMENTS

★

I WOULD LIKE TO THANK the following people, whose guidance, encouragement, and support played an important part in the writing of this book: Mary Evans and Jill Bialosky, agent and editor, Elaina Richardson and the Corporation of Yaddo, Alexander Chancellor, Roger Angell, Nancy Novograd, Larry Colan, William Gifford, Connie Rosenblum, Willard Spiegleman, Phillip Lopate, Joanna Yas, Hava Kohav Beller, Alexander Beller, Lisolette Bendix Stern, Max M. Stern, Penny Riegleman, Bryan Charles, Sabin Streeter, Scott Smith, Steven Perrine, The Writers Room, Evan Carver, Stanley Bosworth, and my very special Elizabeth.